24.95

ENTIALS Books

**Essentials for the N**... ...eally Need to Know in a Nutshell (Aktan)

**Essentials for the A&E NURSE:** Emergency Department Orientation in a Nutshell (Buettner)

**Essentials About GI AND LIVER DISEASES FOR NURSES:** What APRNs Need to Know in a Nutshell (Chaney)

**Essentials on COMBATTING NURSE BULLYING, INCIVILITY, AND WORKPLACE VIOLENCE:** What Nurses Need to Know in a Nutshell (Ciocco)

**Essentials for the THEATRE NURSE:** An Orientation and Care Guide in a Nutshell (Criscitelli)

**Essentials for the NEONATAL NURSE:** A Nursing Orientation and Care Guide in a Nutshell (Davidson)

**Essentials for the LONG-TERM CARE NURSE:** What Nursing Home and Assisted Living Nurses Need to Know in a Nutshell (Eliopoulos)

**Essentials for the CLINICAL NURSE MANAGER:** Managing a Changing Workplace in a Nutshell (Fry)

**Essentials for EVIDENCE-BASED PRACTICE:** Implementing EBP in a Nutshell (Godshall)

**Essentials for Nurses About HOME INFUSION THERAPY:** The Expert's Best Practice Guide in a Nutshell (Gorski)

**Essentials for MIDWIVES:** Labour & Delivery Orientation in a Nutshell (Groll)

**Essentials for the RADIOLOGY NURSE:** An Orientation and Nursing Care Guide in a Nutshell (Grossman)

**Essentials for the CARDIAC SURGERY NURSE:** Caring for Cardiac Surgery Patients in a Nutshell (Hodge)

**Essentials for DEMENTIA CARE:** What Nurses Need to Know in a Nutshell (Miller)

**Essentials for STROKE CARE NURSING:** An Expert Guide in a Nutshell (Morrison)

**Essentials for the PAEDIATRIC NURSE:** An Orientation Guide in a Nutshell (Rupert, Young)

**Essentials for the TRIAGE NURSE:** An Orientation and Care Guide in a Nutshell (Visser, Montejano, Grossman)

**Essentials for the HOSPICE NURSE:** A Concise Guide to End-of-Life Care (Wright)

**Essentials About PTSD:** A Guide for Nurses and Other Health Care Professionals (Adams)

**Essentials for the CLINICAL NURSING INSTRUCTOR:** Clinical Teaching in a Nutshell (Kan, Stabler-Haas)

**Essentials for MANAGING PATIENTS WITH A PSYCHIATRIC DISORDER:** What RNs, NPs, and New Psych Nurses Need to Know (Marshall)

**Essentials About the GYNAECOLOGIC EXAM:** A Professional Guide for NPs, PAs, and Midwives (Secor, Fantasia)

# ESSENTIALS FOR
# THE CARDIAC SURGERY NURSE

**Tanya Hodge, MS, RN, CNS, CCRN, CNRN,** is a cardiovascular clinical nurse specialist, certified critical care nurse, and certified neuroscience registered nurse. She worked clinically in a variety of cardiac-related settings, including cardiac telemetry, transplant/metabolic clinical nursing, cardiology intensive care nursing, and cardiovascular research at University of California–Davis Medical Center. She was a cardio vascular CNS at Mercy General Hospital in Sacramento, California, between 2007 and 2013. Since 2013, she has worked as nurse manager of the Cardiac Interventional Unit and Progressive Care Unit and, most recently, the Medical/Surgical/Neuro Intensive Care Unit at Mercy General. She is a member of the American Association of Critical Care Nurses and the American Association of Neuroscience Nurses.

# ESSENTIALS FOR THE CARDIAC SURGERY NURSE

## Caring for Cardiac Surgery Patients in a Nutshell

Tanya Hodge, MS, RN, CNS, CCRN, CNRN

SPRINGER PUBLISHING COMPANY
NEW YORK

Copyright © 2016 Springer Publishing Company, LLC

Springer Publishing Company, LLC
11 West 42nd Street
New York, NY 10036
www.springerpub.com

*Acquisitions Editor*: Joseph Morita
*Production Editor*: Kris Parrish
*Composition*: S4Carlisle Publishing Services

*ISBN*: 978-0-8261-7269-3

15 16 17 18 19 / 5 4 3 2 1

The author and the publisher of this Work have made every effort to use sources believed to be reliable to provide information that is accurate and compatible with the standards generally accepted at the time of publication. Because medical science is continually advancing, our knowledge base continues to expand. Therefore, as new information becomes available, changes in procedures become necessary. We recommend that the reader always consult current research and specific institutional policies before performing any clinical procedure. The author and publisher shall not be liable for any special, consequential, or exemplary damages resulting, in whole or in part, from the readers' use of, or reliance on, the information contained in this book. The publisher has no responsibility for the persistence or accuracy of URLs for external or third-party Internet websites referred to in this publication and does not guarantee that any content on such websites is, or will remain, accurate or appropriate.

Special discounts on bulk quantities of our books are available to corporations, professional associations, pharmaceutical companies, health care organizations, and other qualifying groups. If you are interested in a custom book, including chapters from more than one of our titles, we can provide that service as well.

**For details, please contact:**
Special Sales Department, Springer Publishing Company, LLC
11 West 42nd Street, 15th Floor, New York, NY 10036-8002
Phone: 877-687-7476 or 212-431-4370; Fax: 212-941-7842
E-mail: sales@springerpub.com

The ESSENTIALS series was published in the United States by Springer Publishing Company, LLC, as the FAST FACTS series.

# Contents

## Part IV: Extended Postoperative Period

## Part V: Long-Term Recovery

# Preface

Because of advances in technology over the years, many patients who used to undergo cardiac surgery are now treated in the cardiac catheterization lab. This means that the patients who now have cardiac surgery are often older and sicker than those who had cardiac surgery in the past. Today's patients have more comorbidities and are at higher risk of complications, making it increasingly important to have knowledgeable and skilled nurses caring for them.

While reflecting on this book, I realized that several important inclusions advance the knowledge base of nurses caring for cardiac surgery patients. To that end, I included a section on congenital heart disease in adults. More people with congenital heart disease are living to adulthood, and their care requires additional knowledge. The section on ventricular assist and other support devices is robust, because these are increasingly being used in cardiac surgery programs. The chapters reflect the most recent clinical practice guidelines and include such topics as implications for patients taking newer anticoagulants. Modifications to the content were made before publication to ensure the book would be more helpful to the bedside nurse.

The book has a chapter dedicated to stroke in cardiac surgery patients. This complication is increasingly common, and recognition and appropriate treatment is essential for these patients. Cardiac nurses are often unaware of the critical importance of the actions of the bedside nurse in this patient population. This chapter outlines actions to take, and what to look for, to give cardiac surgery patients who experience a stroke the best possible chance of achieving a good functional outcome.

*Tanya Hodge*

# Acknowledgments

Projects like this book cannot be accomplished alone. There are so many people who helped and supported me. I want to say "thank you" to the following: my husband, Shad, and my two daughters, Molly and Cora, who supported me and gave me the "alone time" to write; my coworkers at Mercy General Hospital, especially Patty Garrity-Jasper, who encouraged me along the way, and Robyn Stillian, who helped me with the new chapter on stroke; the nurses I currently work with in the Medical/Surgical/Neuro Intensive Care Unit, who have taught me so much about teamwork, empathy, and caring for patients; and all of my colleagues in Cardiovascular Services, who care for hundreds of cardiac patients every month, seeing all of the amazing successes as well as the complications. For all of them, and for cardiac nurses in other institutions, this book was written.

# Preoperative Period

## Overview, Assessment, and Surgery Prep Guidelines

# Epidemiology of Coronary Artery Disease, Valve Disease, and Need for Heart Surgery

*Heart disease is one of the most common causes of death in the world. Symptoms may begin gradually, but for many people severe symptoms strike suddenly. Nurses need to be aware of the symptoms of and treatments available for heart disease to manage patients with both slowly progressive disease and disease with sudden onset.*

## Objectives

In this chapter, you will learn:

1. The symptoms of coronary artery disease and acute coronary syndrome
2. When someone with coronary artery disease would need coronary artery bypass graft surgery
3. When disease of the cardiac valves would require surgery
4. Key points in caring for patients with congenital heart disease

## CORONARY ARTERY DISEASE

Coronary artery disease (CAD) is one of the leading deadly diseases in the world. It is estimated that each year in the United

States alone, over 780,000 people experience acute coronary syndrome (ACS). About 70% of these will experience non–ST segment elevation ACS (Amsterdam et al.). In 2009, 386,324 Americans died of CAD, which was approximately 1 out of every 6 deaths in the United States (Go et al., 2013). If recognized and treated early, long-term damage from myocardial infarction (MI) and ischemia can be prevented or made less severe.

## Symptoms of CAD

CAD is the buildup of plaque consisting of fatty material and inflammatory cells inside the wall of one or more coronary arteries (Figure 1.1). As the disease progresses and these plaques grow in size, they begin to weaken the wall of the artery and grow into the lumen of the artery. Calcium may be deposited in large plaques, hardening them, and they often become large enough to impede the flow of blood. Most people who have CAD are unaware that they have this disease until they experience symptoms. Symptoms of CAD are related to a lack of blood flow to the heart muscle (ischemia) and are called anginal symptoms or angina. Traditionally, chest pain and chest pressure were considered the primary anginal symptoms, often accompanied by pain radiating to the jaw or arm, nausea, diaphoresis, or shortness of breath. It is now recognized that many people, especially women, diabetics, and the elderly, may experience atypical symptoms. These are symptoms that generally occur without chest pain or pressure and may include unexplained weakness or fatigue, nausea, indigestion, dizziness, or back pain (Jacobson, Marzlin, & Webner, 2007).

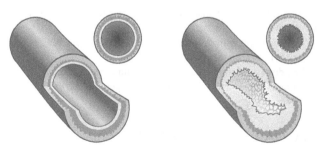

**FIGURE 1.1**  Atherosclerosis.

Stable angina refers to symptoms that occur with physical exertion or stress and subside with rest. Typically, these stable symptoms are caused by the slow buildup of atherosclerotic plaque in the walls of the coronary arteries. As the arteries narrow, they are not able to supply sufficient blood to meet the increased demand during exercise or other stresses that increase the heart rate. Once the heart rate slows (usually during rest), oxygen demand decreases and symptoms subside. Symptoms that do not subside with rest may signal a more deadly progression of CAD: ACS.

_ESSENTIAL FACTS_

Ischemia from CAD is caused by a mismatch between oxygen supply and oxygen demand. The resulting myocardial ischemia may cause a variety of symptoms.

## ACUTE CORONARY SYNDROME

CAD often begins years before ACS strikes. An inflammatory process causes plaque to build up in the coronary arteries. People with certain risk factors, as noted in Table 1.1, are more likely to have plaque buildup, especially if their diagnoses are severe or if more than one risk factors is present. As the buildup process evolves, the plaque may become unstable and prone to rupture. If a coronary artery plaque ruptures, the inflammatory cells in the plaque cause platelets to be activated, triggering the clotting cascade, which causes formation of a clot in the artery. The severity of the episode and amount of damage to the heart muscle depend on the extent of the clot.

ACS is a spectrum of diseases, including unstable angina (USA), non–ST segment elevation myocardial infarction (NSTEMI), and ST segment elevation myocardial infarction (STEMI). USA is caused by a thrombus in the coronary artery that resolves spontaneously through the body's own thrombolytic system. If at some point a clot forms and the body is unable to break it apart, USA progresses to either NSTEMI or STEMI.

### TABLE 1.1 Risk Factors for CAD

Nonmodifiable risk factors:
- Family history—premature CAD (younger than 55 in men and younger than 65 in women) in a first-degree relative (mother, father, sibling)
- Older age (over 65)
- Gender—men are at higher risk than women until women reach menopause

Modifiable risk factors:
- Cigarette smoking
- Dyslipidemia
- Hypertension
- Diabetes mellitus
- Abdominal obesity
- Lack of physical activity
- Low daily fruit and vegetable consumption
- Overconsumption of alcohol
- Psychosocial risk factors—stress, depression, anxiety, anger, and hostility

CAD, coronary artery disease.

*Source:* Jacobson et al. (2007).

## ESSENTIAL FACTS

ACS is a sudden and life-threatening event caused by rupture of an unstable atherosclerotic plaque. The resulting blood clot in the artery causes myocardial ischemia or infarction, or both, depending on the amount of blood flow that is occluded.

## Unstable Angina

USA occurs when a clot occludes or partially occludes a coronary artery, then is broken down by the body's fibrinolytic system, restoring blood flow. Anginal symptoms occur, and then subside. Symptoms may occur at rest or with minimal exertion and typically last more than 20 minutes. These anginal symptoms tend to recur, often with increasing severity and frequency.

# Non–ST Segment Elevation Myocardial Infarction

NSTEMI refers to a clot that has partially occluded a coronary artery causing anginal symptoms. Some blood continues to reach the myocardium, but it provides an insufficient supply of oxygen and nutrients to the cells. This results in ischemia, which may be detected by changes such as ST depression or T-wave inversion on a 12-lead electrocardiogram (ECG), by an increase in cardiac enzymes, or both.

# ST Segment Elevation Myocardial Infarction

If the clot completely blocks the flow of blood to the myocardium, the result is STEMI. The blockage of blood flow causes ischemia at first, then necrosis (death of myocardial cells). As cardiac muscle cells die, they no longer conduct electrical current, which results in elevation of ST segments on a 12-lead ECG. (See Table 1.2 for information on how to determine which artery is blocked by looking at the 12-lead ECG.) The death of myocardial cells also causes enzymes, normally found inside these muscle cells, to be released into the bloodstream. This leads to an increase in cardiac enzymes in the bloodstream. (See Table 1.3 for onset time of commonly measured cardiac enzymes.)

## ESSENTIAL FACTS

Patients with STEMI need to have the occluded artery opened emergently to save the heart muscle. Thrombolytics should be administered within 30 minutes of the patient's arrival (door to drug time). If angioplasty and stenting will be used, the artery must be opened within 90 minutes (door to balloon time).

# Treatment of Acute Coronary Syndrome

Treatment of ACS involves administering medications, evaluating the extent of the disease, and restoring blood flow to ischemic areas of the heart.

## TABLE 1.2 Coronary Arteries and Corresponding ECG Leads

| Coronary Artery | ECG Lead | Location of Myocardial Infarction |
| --- | --- | --- |
| RCA | II, III, aVF | Inferior |
| LAD | V1, V2 | Septal |
| | V1, V2, V3, V4 | Anterior |
| LCx | I, aVL, V5, V6 | Lateral |

LAD, left anterior descending; LCx, left circumflex; RCA, right coronary artery.

## TABLE 1.3 Onset, Peak, and Duration of Serum Cardiac Enzyme Levels After an Ischemic Episode

| Marker or Enzyme | Starts to Rise (Hours) | Peaks (Hours) | Returns to Normal (Days) |
| --- | --- | --- | --- |
| Creatine kinase (CK total) | 2–6 | 18–36 | 3–6 |
| Creatine kinase–MB (CK-MB) | 4–8 | 18–24 | 3 |
| Troponin–I | 3 | 10–24 | 7–10 |
| Troponin–T | 3 | 10–24 | 10–14 |
| Myoglobin | 2–3 | 6–9 | 1–2 |

## Medications Used in Acute Coronary Syndrome

As described above, patients with ACS have a thrombus partially or completely occluding a coronary artery. Medications are aimed at preventing further growth of the clot, shrinking the clot, and minimizing damage done by ischemia. A patient presenting with symptoms of ACS should immediately be given an aspirin and placed on oxygen, as ordered by a physician. Aspirin is an antiplatelet medication that slows the growth of the thrombus. Administering oxygen increases the supply of oxygen available in the blood for ischemic tissues. Nitroglycerin administered sublingually is quickly absorbed into the bloodstream. The vasodilatory effect of nitroglycerin allows increased blood flow to ischemic areas. If chest pain or other anginal symptoms are not relieved with three doses of nitroglycerin, morphine should be given, per physician's order. Morphine simultaneously calms the patient, decreasing oxygen demand, and dilates coronary arteries to increase blood supply.

**CLINICAL ALERT!** Caution should be used when administering nitroglycerin and morphine. Neither should be given if the systolic blood pressure is below 90 mmHg. Nitroglycerin should not be given if the patient has taken medications for erectile dysfunction, as the combination may cause dangerously low blood pressure.

## Evaluating Coronary Artery Disease

When patients are experiencing ACS, it is important to determine the extent of CAD. Most patients who present with ACS need to undergo angiography to definitively determine how much CAD is present and decide on treatment. (See Chapter 2 for a description of coronary angiography.)

## Revascularization

Patients who have a thrombus completely occluding a coronary artery (STEMI) need immediate treatment to open the blocked artery. This can be done using medications or in the cardiac cath lab with percutaneous coronary intervention (PCI).

Thrombolytics may be used to open an occluded artery. Tenecteplase (TNK) is a commonly used thrombolytic for STEMI and must be ordered by a physician. Patients need to be screened prior to administration of thrombolytics due to high risk of bleeding. Thrombolytics are contraindicated in patients who have recently had a stroke or major trauma, who have severe uncontrolled hypertension, or have suspected aortic dissection. Extreme caution should be used when administering a thrombolytic to a patient who has had recent gastrointestinal bleeding or recent major surgery, or one who is taking anticoagulants. If a patient experiencing STEMI is to receive a thrombolytic, the medication should be given as soon as possible. The goal for of thrombolytic treatment in patients with STEMI is to administer within 30 minutes of presentation to an emergency department.

It is the responsibility of the physician ordering the thrombolytic to screen patients for contraindications. However, nurses need to be aware of the contraindications and notify the physician if any are present; the nurse may have information not available to the physician. Nurses should not administer a medication that is contraindicated.

Hospitals with a cardiac cath lab and the ability to perform cardiac interventions should use PCI, when possible, to open the artery of a patient experiencing STEMI. PCI includes thrombectomy (directly removing the clot using a catheter in the coronary artery), angioplasty (inflating a balloon at the end of a catheter in the area of occlusion in the coronary artery), and stenting (placing a small tube of metal in the coronary artery to hold the artery open). The goal for patients with STEMI should be to have the artery open within 90 minutes of presentation to an emergency department.

## Need for Surgery

Patients with a small number of focal coronary artery lesions and those that are easily reached using PCI are usually treated using angioplasty and stenting. A catheter is threaded through an artery (usually femoral or radial) and pushed forward until it is advanced into the diseased coronary artery. A balloon at the end of the catheter is inflated at the site of the coronary artery plaque and essentially smashes the plaque against the walls of the artery to increase the size of the lumen of the artery. This catheter is removed and a second catheter is advanced to the same place. At the end of this catheter is a small tube of metal called a stent (Figure 1.2). As the balloon at the end of the catheter is inflated, the stent expands to the size of the artery and holds the artery open. The stent remains in place and the catheter is removed.

Many patients who have multiple lesions or diffuse disease (narrowing of a significant portion of the coronary arteries) need

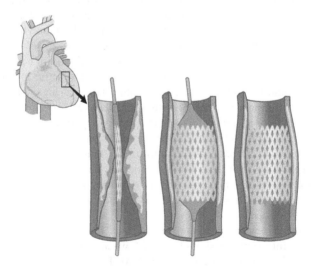

**FIGURE 1.2** Percutaneous coronary intervention—stent placement.

surgical repair with coronary artery bypass grafting (CABG). Also, patients who have valve disease or other structural heart disease that requires surgical repair typically have CABG at the time of valve repair rather than undergoing PCI for CAD (see Table 1.4). An interventional cardiologist and cardiac surgeon should review the films and clinical presentation of patients with complicated disease or anatomy to determine, with the input of the patient, the best strategy for revascularization (Hillis et al., 2011).

Nurses play an important role in reinforcing the rationale for PCI versus cardiac surgery. An understanding of the rationale for each helps nurses as they educate patients and prepare them for surgery or other treatments.

## ESSENTIAL FACTS

The choice between catheter-based intervention for CAD and heart surgery is based on the patient's overall clinical picture, extent of the disease, presence of other heart disease, and comorbidities.

### TABLE 1.4 Indications for Percutaneous Coronary Intervention and Coronary Artery Bypass Grafting

| Indications for PCI | Indications for CABG |
|---|---|
| • Focal lesions in one or two vessels<br>• One- or two-vessel disease with good left ventricular function<br>  ■ Left main stenosis of > 50% with low risk for PCI procedural complications and high risk for surgical complications<br>  ■ Patients experiencing STEMI when PCI can be done more quickly and safely than CABG | • Left main disease (> 50% occluded) or significant (> 70% occluded) stenoses in three major coronary arteries<br>• A large amount of ischemic heart muscle<br>• Diffuse multivessel disease<br>• Multivessel disease in the presence of diabetes or poor left ventricular function (ejection fraction < 50%)<br>• Failed PCI<br>• Presence of CAD when other heart surgery is indicated |

CABG, coronary artery bypass grafting; CAD, coronary artery disease; PCI, percutaneous coronary intervention; STEMI, ST segment elevation myocardial infarction.

*Source:* Hillis et al. (2011).

# VALVE DISEASE

Disease of one of the heart valves frequently requires cardiac surgery to repair or replace the valve. Valve disease may be caused by rheumatic fever, infective endocarditis, calcification, trauma, or connective tissue disorders such as Marfan syndrome. The aortic and mitral valves are most commonly affected and cause the most symptoms.

Normal valves maintain the forward flow of blood in the heart. When diseased, valves may become stenotic (unable to open fully, preventing the forward flow of blood) or regurgitant, incompetent, or insufficient (unable to close fully, allowing blood to flow backward); see Table 1.5.

## Mitral Stenosis

Mitral stenosis (MS) occurs more frequently in women than in men. When diseased, valve leaflets become thick and fibrous,

**TABLE 1.5 Mitral and Aortic Valve Disease**

| Disease | Signs and Symptoms | Indications for Surgery |
|---------|--------------------|--------------------------|
| MS | Dyspnea on exertion, fatigue, edema, tricuspid regurgitation | Patients with moderate or severe MS who are symptomatic or have severe pulmonary hypertension |
| MR | Heart failure, atrial fibrillation | Severe MR with symptoms of left ventricular dysfunction or enlargement or with new-onset atrial fibrillation |
| AS | Angina, syncope, sudden cardiac death, heart failure, systolic murmur in the aortic position | Severe AS with symptoms of left ventricular dysfunction. Severe or moderate AS in patients undergoing coronary artery bypass grafting (CABG) or other heart surgery |
| AI | Heart failure, diastolic blowing murmur | Severe AI with symptoms of left ventricular dysfunction or enlargement. Severe or moderate AI in patients undergoing CABG or other heart surgery |

AI, aortic insufficiency; AS, aortic stenosis; CABG, coronary artery bypass grafting; MR, mitral regurgitation; MS, mitral stenosis.

producing a narrowed valve opening and impeding blood flow from the left atrium to the left ventricle. Pressure builds and the left atrium dilates, often leading to atrial fibrillation. The increased pressure in the left atrium backs up into the pulmonary circulation, causing pulmonary hypertension and congestion.

## Mitral Regurgitation

Mitral regurgitation (MR) occurs when the valve leaflets do not close fully, allowing blood to move backward from the left ventricle into the left atrium. This may occur acutely, such as with the rupture of cordae tendineae or with trauma. MR may also occur chronically over time as a result of degenerative disorders, such as rheumatic fever. MR may also occur secondary to left ventricular dilation, when the valve opening enlarges.

With MR, blood moves backward during systole into the left atrium, increasing pressure in that atrium. This may dilate the left atrium and cause pulmonary congestion. Left atrial dilation may also cause atrial fibrillation. During diastole, there is more volume than usual in the left atrium, which in turn flows into the left ventricle. This continual increase in volume in the left ventricle leads to ventricular dilation and hypertrophy. Over time, this results in heart failure. If MR occurs acutely, the left atrium and ventricle do not have time to compensate for the increase in volume. The sudden increase in volume and pressure result in sudden pulmonary congestion and edema.

## Aortic Stenosis

Aortic stenosis (AS) is caused by obstruction of blood as it moves from the left ventricle into the aorta. The most common cause is calcification, which occurs in some people older than 60 due to aging. The valve cusps become increasingly less mobile over a period of years, during which time the person is asymptomatic. The left ventricle has to work harder to move blood out into the aorta, and left ventricular hypertrophy occurs, eventually leading to heart failure. As the aortic valve area becomes smaller, pressure builds and blood backs up into the left atrium, worsening any underlying MR. Patients may present with angina or syncope, or both.

## Aortic Insufficiency

In aortic insufficiency (AI), regurgitation of blood from the aorta back into the left ventricle may be caused by an abnormality in the valve leaflets or by dilation of the aortic root. The backward flow of blood causes volume overload in the ventricle. In chronic, progressive disease states, the left ventricle becomes hypertrophied due to increased volume and pressure over time. The disease may remain asymptomatic until heart failure develops. If the AI occurs acutely, the left ventricle does not have time to compensate and sudden volume overload leads to acute heart failure and pulmonary edema.

## *ESSENTIAL FACTS*

Patients with multivessel, severe, or diffuse CAD are usually referred for heart surgery. Patients needing repair or replacement of heart valves are referred for cardiac surgery, and CAD is treated at the same time.

## CONGENITAL HEART DISEASE

Congenital heart disease (CHD) refers to a wide variety of structural issues present from birth. Surgical repair strategies have improved to such as extent that more than 80% of patients have survived to adulthood since the 1970s (Kouchoukos, Blackstone, Hanley, & Kirklin, 2013). It has been estimated that approximately 800,000 adults in the United States have CHD. Some patients present for care as adults with primary CHD, meaning that it has not been previously treated. This may be because it was minor enough to escape detection until adulthood, because it is an anomaly with a relatively benign pathophysiology, or because it was too complicated to treat in childhood. Also, patients who grew up in countries without advanced pediatric CHD management may emigrate or travel to a country with advanced treatment opportunities in adulthood. Secondary CHD refers to CHD that has previously been treated (Kouchoukos et al., 2013). (See Table 1.6 for examples of CHD.)

Although a detailed description of these defects and the care for this patient population is outside the scope of this book, it is

## TABLE 1.6 Types of Congenital Heart Disease in Adults

- Low complexity—newly diagnosed
  - Isolated congenital aortic valve disease
  - Isolated congenital mitral valve disease
  - Small ASD
  - Isolated small VSD
  - Mild pulmonary stenosis
  - Small PDA

- Low complexity—repaired
  - Previously ligated or occluded PDA
  - Repaired ASD
  - Repaired VSD

- Moderate complexity
  - Aorto-left ventricular fistulas
  - Anomalous pulmonary venous drainage
  - Complex atrioventricular septal defects
  - Coarctation of the aorta (Figure 1.3)
  - Unrepaired PDA
  - Moderate to severe pulmonary valve regurgitation or stenosis
  - Subvalvular AS
  - Tetralogy of Fallot (Figure 1.4)
  - VSD with other major anomalies

- Great complexity
  - Cyanotic heart disease (all forms)
  - Double-outlet ventricle
  - Eisenmenger syndrome
  - Fontan procedure
  - Single ventricle
  - Pulmonary atresia
  - Pulmonary vascular obstructive disease
  - Transposition of the great arteries
  - Tricuspid atresia
  - Truncus arteriosus or hemitruncus
  - Other abnormalities of atrioventricular or ventriculoarterial connection

ASD, atrial septal defect; AS, aortic stenosis; PDA, patent ductus arteriosus; VSD, ventricular septal defect.

Adapted from Kouchoukos et al. (2013).

important for nurses working with cardiac surgery patients to be aware of some key points related to CHD.

- Patients with complex CHD should be followed up frequently by a health care provider specifically trained in caring for adults

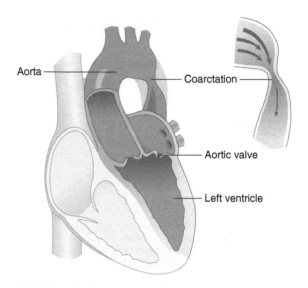

**FIGURE 1.3** Coarctation of the aorta.

with CHD. Patients with complex CHD admitted to a hospital should, after medical stabilization, be transferred to a regional adult CHD center.

- Newer devices and techniques allow for treatment of patent ductus arteriosus (PDA), most atrial septal defects (ASDs), and some ventricular septal defects (VSDs) in the cath lab in a minimally invasive manner. In addition, coarctation of the aorta is often now treated percutaneously with balloon dilation and stenting (Burke, 2012). Cardiac surgeons increasingly en-counter devices that have previously been used to repair CHD. This includes stents found in the aorta and pulmonary arteries as well as atrial and ventricular septal occlusion devices used to close PDAs or septal defects. This can complicate future treatments.

- Patients with previously repaired CHD may have had multiple surgeries during childhood and into adulthood. Repeat cardiac surgeries are extremely difficult, because of significant scar tis-sue and adhesions. Repeat sternotomy carries a higher risk of hemorrhage and air embolism. In addition, abnormal anatomy may place the heart in a slightly different position in the chest and directly against the sternum, increasing the risk of damage

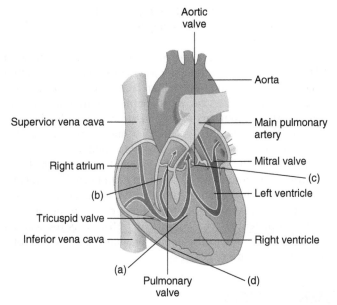

**FIGURE 1.4** Tetralogy of Fallot: (a) Ventricular septal defect—a hole between the right and left ventricles. (b) Pulmonary infundibular stenosis—narrowing of the right ventricular outflow tract, either at or just below the pulmonary valve. (c) Overriding aorta—aortic valve connected to both the right and left ventricles. (d) Right ventricular hypertrophy—thickening of the wall of the right ventricle (this is the most common cyanotic congenital heart defect).

to the heart during incision. Femoral arteries may have scar tissue or even be completely occluded due to repeated access for cardiac catheterization or surgeries.

- Patients with CHD are at risk for several complications throughout their lives. A number of syndromes associated with CHD (e.g., Down syndrome) include neurological, developmental, and cognitive deficits. Many of these syndromes are associated with disease processes in other organ systems as well. Previously undiagnosed CHD often becomes symptomatic during pregnancy, with potentially serious implications to the mortality and morbidity of both the mother and fetus. Patients with complex CHD, previously repaired or not, are at higher risk of heart failure, especially later in life. Large, untreated left-to-right shunts may lead to irreversible pulmonary hypertension.

- Arrhythmias are a huge concern in these patients. Adults with CHD are at risk for developing a wide variety of conduction delays and atrial and ventricular tachyarrhythmias (Burke, 2012). Atrial flutter is the most common arrhythmia seen in this population, but any other arrhythmia may also be seen (Kouchoukos et al., 2013). There are many possible reasons, including surgical scar tissue, ischemic insults, pressure and volume overload, and cyanosis. Pacemaker and defibrillator insertions in these patients are often complicated by unusual anatomical pathways and stenotic veins. In patients with cyanotic CHD, arrhythmias are the leading contributing cause of death. In patients with noncyanotic CHD, MI is the leading cause of death, due to the impact of acquired atherosclerotic heart disease (Burke, 2012).

## *ESSENTIAL FACTS*

There is an increasing population of adult patients with CHD as a result of improvements in surgeries and treatments in childhood. Arrhythmias are the most common complication seen in adults with CHD, and treatment of arrhythmias and other conditions may be complicated by previous surgeries and abnormal cardiac and vascular anatomy.

## REFERENCES

Amsterdam, E. A., Wenger, N. K., Brindis, R. G., Casey, D. E., Ganiats, T. G., Holmes, D.R., Jr., . . . Zieman, S.J. (2014). AHA/ACC guideline for the management of patients with non-ST elevation acute coronary syndromes. *Journal of the American College of Cardiology, 64*(24):2645–2687.

Burke, R. P. (2012). Surgery for adult congenital heart disease. In L. H. Cohn (Ed.), *Cardiac surgery in the adult* (4th ed.). New York, NY: McGraw-Hill Medical.

Go, A. S., Mozaffarian, D., Rojer, V. L., Benjamin, E. J., Berry, J. D., Borden, W. B. . . . American Heart Association Statistical Committee and Stroke Statistics Subcommittee. (2013). Heart disease and stroke statistics—2013 update: A report from the American Heart Association. *Circulation, 127,* e6–e245.

Hillis, L. D. , Smith, P. K., Anderson, J. L., Bittl, J. A., Bridges, C. R., Byrne, J. G., . . . Winniford, M. D. (2011). 2011 ACCF/AHA guideline for coronary artery bypass graft surgery: A report of the American College of Cardiology Foundation/American Heart Association Task Force on Practice Guidelines. *Journal of the American College of Cardiology, 58,* e123–e210.

Jacobson, C., Marzlin, K., & Webner, C. (2007). *Cardiovascular nursing practice.* Burien, WA: Cardiovascular Nursing Education Associates.

Kouchoukos, N. T., Blackstone, E. H., Hanley, F. L., & Kirklin, J. K. (2013). *Kirklin/Barratt-Boyes cardiac surgery* (4th ed.). Philadelphia, PA: Elsevier Saunders.

# 2

## Diagnostic Tests

*Diagnostic testing can determine the type and extent of heart disease and guide treatment strategies. Since complications can occur with most diagnostic tests, the least invasive test is used first when possible. The most invasive tests generally give the most information about cardiac disease. Patients need to understand the reasons for diagnostic tests and what to expect during the test.*

### Objectives

In this chapter, you will learn:

1. Some of the noninvasive tests used to evaluate a patient for coronary artery disease
2. Noninvasive tests used to evaluate valve function
3. What information is gathered during a cardiac catheterization

## NONINVASIVE TESTING TO DETECT CORONARY ARTERY DISEASE

Noninvasive testing strategies carry the least risk for patients, but there is the possibility for false positives and false negatives.

Noninvasive tests involve two parts: stressing the heart and imaging the heart. The stress portion may involve either exercise or medications to increase heart rate and oxygen demand. The imaging portion may involve electrocardiography (ECG), echocardiography (echo), or nuclear imaging.

## ESSENTIAL FACTS

A positive noninvasive test is an indication for a more invasive test, usually cardiac catheterization.

### Exercise Treadmill Test and Exercise Stress Echo

An exercise treadmill test involves having a patient follow a specified, graded protocol on a treadmill to stress the heart; a continuous 12-lead ECG is used to evaluate the heart for ischemic changes. Ischemic changes occur in the distribution of the affected coronary artery.

An exercise stress echo includes exercise on a treadmill and a continuous 12-lead ECG, and adds evaluation of wall motion. An echo is obtained before and again during exercise to determine changes in response to elevated heart rate. If an artery is occluded enough to limit blood flow, stress on the heart from exercise will cause wall motion irregularities in the area fed by that artery. If the patient is unable to exercise, dobutamine may be used to stress the heart in place of exercise (dobutamine stress echo).

▶ **NURSING IMPLICATIONS:** Patients who will receive a noninvasive test involving exercise should be able and prepared to exercise. Patients who have poor balance or who do not walk well are not good candidates for these tests. Patients should be sent for their test wearing pants and supportive shoes, if possible.

### Myocardial Perfusion Imaging

Patients who undergo nuclear perfusion imaging are injected with radioactive tracers, which can be detected as they are "taken up" by the heart muscle. The most common tracers include thallium-201, technetium-99m sestamibi (Cardiolite), and technetium-99m tetrofosmin (Myoview). The tracer is injected during peak exercise and imaging is performed. The agents are taken up into viable myocardium and these areas light up on the imaging scan. Infarcted or dead myocardium remains dark. Myocardium that is ischemic may have a delay in the uptake of tracer, so images are taken a short time later to evaluate redistribution of the tracer. Patients who cannot exercise are given a medication such as adenosine or dipyridamole (Persantine) to mimic the effect of exercise on blood flow in the heart.

▶ **NURSING IMPLICATIONS:** Patients need to understand that they will need to lie still while images are being taken. Patients should be reassured that they will receive only a very small amount of radiation during the test.

## Computed Tomography and Magnetic Resonance Imaging

CT is used primarily for evaluating diseases of the aorta. New advances in CT scanning hold promise for evaluation of coronary artery disease. Electron beam CT can give information about coronary calcification, which is associated with the presence of coronary artery plaques. This is typically done to screen asymptomatic patients. Use of a multislice CT with contrast (CT angiography [CTA]) can give information about specific coronary arteries and can identify coronary artery narrowing. Until recently, there has been little evidence in the literature about the clinical outcomes associated with noninvasive testing in patients with symptoms suggesting CAD. A recent randomized study showed no difference in clinical outcomes between CTA and three common functional tests (exercise treadmill test, exercise stress echo, and myocardial perfusion imaging; Douglas et al., 2015).

Like CT scanning, MRI technology is improving and becoming more versatile. MRI is primarily used to evaluate diseases of the aorta and pericardium. This test is also useful to detect masses and other irregularities. When contrast dye is used (magnetic resonance angiography), occlusions in the proximal coronary arteries may be detected.

# DIAGNOSTIC TESTING TO DETECT VALVE DISEASE

## Echocardiogram (Echo)

An echocardiogram is an ultrasound of the heart that provides two- and three-dimensional moving pictures and gives much valuable information about the structures of the heart, wall motion and ventricular function, and blood flow. This test may be done via the transthoracic (ultrasound probe is on the external chest wall) or transesophageal (ultrasound probe is placed inside the esophagus at the level of the heart) method. A transesophageal echocardiogram (TEE) provides the most detailed information about valve function because, in the esophagus, the probe is very close to the heart. An echo and TEE are frequently performed before, during, and after heart surgery to evaluate valve and ventricular function.

▶ **NURSING IMPLICATIONS:** Patients who undergo an echo should understand that it is a noninvasive ultrasound of the heart. A TEE should be explained fully so patients understand that it will be uncomfortable and that sedation will be used.

## *ESSENTIAL FACTS*

Patients undergoing a TEE require sedation as the probe is passed into the esophagus and images are taken.

## CARDIAC CATHETERIZATION

Cardiac catheterization (cardiac cath) remains the gold standard test for evaluating coronary arteries. During a cardiac cath, information may also be obtained about valve function, wall motion, and ejection fraction.

Cardiac cath is recommended prior to most surgical and interventional procedures. Exceptions include certain types of aortic dissections and aortic valve endocarditis since there is significant risk of damage from the catheter if these conditions are present.

## Right Heart Catheterization

During a right heart cath, a pulmonary artery catheter is advanced through a vein into the right atrium, right ventricle, and pulmonary artery. Pressures and oxygen saturations can be measured. Normal pressures are listed in Table 2.1. The tricuspid and pulmonic valves can be evaluated by measuring the pressure gradient across the valves. The pressure gradient is the difference between the pressures on either side of a valve. The greater the difference in pressure, the greater will be the severity of stenosis in that valve. Pulmonary artery pressures can be evaluated when the catheter is in the pulmonary artery. Oxygen saturations can be used to diagnose intracardiac shunts (atrial septal or ventricular septal defects).

**TABLE 2.1  Normal Pressure Measurements During Heart Catheterization**

| Area Measured | Normal Pressures in mmHg |
|---|---|
| Right atrium | Mean 3–8 |
| Right ventricle | Systolic 15–30<br>Diastolic 3–8 |
| Pulmonary artery | Systolic 15–30<br>Diastolic 5–12<br>Mean 9–16 |
| Pulmonary artery in the wedge position | 5–12 |
| Left atrium | 5–12 |
| Left ventricle | Systolic 90–140<br>Diastolic 60–90<br>Mean 70–105 |

## *ESSENTIAL FACTS*

During a right heart catheterization, the venous system is accessed and pressures on the right (venous) side of the heart are measured. The one exception to this is the pulmonary artery wedge pressure, which approximates the pressure in the left atrium if the pulmonary vasculature is normal.

## Left Heart Catheterization

A left heart cath involves advancing a catheter, usually through the femoral or radial artery, into the aorta, left atrium, and left ventricle. Pressures can be measured across the mitral and aortic valves to determine valve function. Dye can be injected into the coronary arteries and various chambers of the heart (left atrium, left ventricle, aortic root and arch) so that structures can be directly visualized.

### *Coronary Angiography*

The coronary arteries originate in the aortic root just above the aortic valve and travel down to supply blood to the heart muscle. To visualize the arteries, the tip of a catheter is placed directly in the proximal opening (ostium) of a coronary artery. Dye is injected and fluoroscopic (x-ray) images are taken of the coronary artery. This gives valuable information about the lumen of the artery, any plaques or occlusions that are present, and the course the artery takes along the surface of the heart. This procedure is done for the native coronary arteries as well as for any grafts that were implanted during previous cardiac surgeries. These images also reveal how well any blockages can be bypassed. Small arteries or arteries with very diffuse distal disease may not be amenable to bypass. The angiogram images and the overall clinical picture of the patient are used to determine the appropriate strategy for treatment (Figure 2.1).

### *Left Ventriculogram and Aortic Root Shot*

A special catheter, called a pigtail, is inserted into the left ventricle. A large amount of dye is injected rapidly into the left ventricle and images are taken as the dye is ejected from the left ventricle. Left ventricular wall motion can be determined and

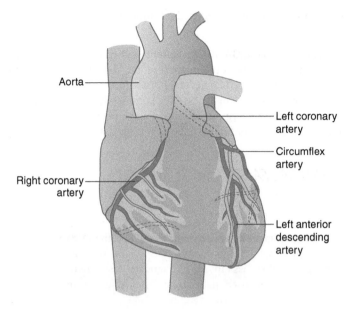

**Figure 2.1** The coronary arteries.

the ejection fraction can be calculated. Any mitral regurgitation will also be seen. The pigtail catheter can be moved up past the aortic valve into the aortic root. Another dye injection reveals the size and shape of the aortic root. The presence of aortic insufficiency will also be detected during the aortic root shot.

## ESSENTIAL FACTS

During a left heart catheterization, the arterial system is accessed via the femoral or radial artery. Dye is injected and the coronary arteries, left ventricle, valves, and aortic root are visualized. Pressures on the left (arterial) side of the heart are measured.

### Detecting Valve Disease

The extent of disease in the mitral and aortic valves can be determined by measuring the pressure gradient across the valves. Valve areas can also be calculated to determine the severity of stenosis in the valve.

▶ **NURSING IMPLICATIONS:** Patients scheduled for a cardiac cath should understand the procedure and that they will need to remain lying flat in bed for several hours after the procedure if the femoral artery is used for access. The contrast dye used in the procedure can cause allergic reactions in some people and can cause renal insufficiency or failure in certain high-risk patients.

## *ESSENTIAL FACTS*

Diagnostic tests are used to determine the extent of coronary artery and valve disease and to determine the appropriate treatment for the disease. Cardiac catheterization and angiography are the gold standard diagnostic tests for this purpose. Often, less invasive diagnostic tests are performed first and, if positive, patients are then referred for cardiac catheterization and angiography.

## REFERENCE

Douglas, P. S., Hoffmann, U., Patel, M. R., Mark, D. B., Al-Khalidi, H. R., Cavanaugh, B., . . . PROMISE Investigators. (2015). Outcomes of anatomical versus functional testing for coronary artery disease. *New England Journal of Medicine, 372*(14), 1291–1300.

# 3

# Preparing a Patient for Cardiac Surgery

*The urgency of cardiac surgery determines how much time is available to prepare the patient. Patients preparing for elective surgery have the most time available. Patients who undergo emergency surgery are often taken directly to the operating room and have little or no preparation for surgery. Preparation time for patients who require urgent surgery varies from several hours to several days. In any of these cases, effort should be made to complete as many of the steps for preparing the patient as time allows. Patients who are fully prepared for surgery have the fewest complications and recover the quickest.*

## Objectives

In this chapter, you will learn:

1. What tests and exams should be completed for patients prior to cardiac surgery
2. How patient and family education can prevent complications after surgery
3. What medications should be given prior to and on the day of surgery

## ESSENTIAL FACTS ====

Patients who undergo urgent or emergent surgery are at highest risk of post-op complications.

## PRE-OP EXAMINATION

Patients who will undergo cardiac surgery need to have a health history taken and a baseline physical exam performed. The health history should include questions about chronic health conditions and prior surgeries. Any history of depression or other psychosocial problems should be noted. Heart and lung sounds should be documented. Neurological status should be assessed. Many patients experience alterations in neurological status after cardiac surgery and an accurate pre-op baseline is important for determining changes. Blood pressure should be taken in both arms. Significant differences in blood pressure between arms can signify subclavian stenosis, which may mean the internal mammary artery cannot be used as a bypass conduit. Smoking history should be documented. Patients who have smoked in the past 6 months are at higher risk for pulmonary complications.

▶ **NURSING IMPLICATIONS:** A thorough pre-op history and exam are important to determine which patients are at higher risk for complications. They are also critical if post-op issues arise and a baseline is needed for comparison.

## ESSENTIAL FACTS ====

Factors that increase post-op mortality and morbidity include respiratory or airway disease, diabetes, obesity, renal failure or dialysis, previous cardiac surgery, low left ventricular ejection fraction, and advanced age (older than 80 years).

### Laboratory Tests

A number of laboratory tests should be completed, including a complete blood count, renal and liver function tests, electrolytes, coagulation panel, and arterial blood gases. A urinalysis is usually completed and often a thyroid panel is drawn. These tests give important information about the patient's risk for complications. Patients with renal or liver disease may need adjustments made to dosages of certain medications. Any infection should be treated prior to surgery whenever possible. Patients with bleeding disorders often require increased use of blood products during and after surgery. Electrolyte abnormalities should be corrected prior to surgery to reduce the risk of arrhythmias. Patients with subclinical hypothyroidism, which occurs without overt symptoms, are more likely to have coronary artery disease. These patients are also more likely to develop certain complications after surgery, such as atrial fibrillation, heart failure, and gastrointestinal complications (Hillis et al., 2011)

▶ **NURSING IMPLICATIONS:** Pre-op laboratory data are critical to determine patients at risk for complications. For example, patients with pre-op renal insufficiency are at much higher risk of developing renal failure after surgery and a urinalysis may uncover a urinary tract infection that needs to be treated prior to surgery.

## Other Diagnostic Tests

A 12-lead electrocardiogram (ECG) should be performed on patients who will undergo cardiac surgery. This provides a baseline for comparison post-op. Patients at high risk of carotid stenosis should undergo a carotid ultrasound prior to cardiac surgery. High-risk attributes include age of more than 65 years, left main coronary stenosis, peripheral arterial disease, history of transient ischemic attack or stroke, hypertension, smoking, and diabetes (Hillis et al., 2011). Severe carotid stenosis, which can be diagnosed by ultrasound, puts patients at high risk of a stroke during cardiac surgery. If severe carotid stenosis is discovered, this should be treated either by carotid endarterectomy or by carotid stenting prior to surgery. Some centers perform carotid endarterectomy in the cardiac operating room immediately before cardiac surgery. (See Chapter 14 for more detailed discussion of stroke.)

## PATIENT AND FAMILY EDUCATION

Pre-op education should include what will happen during surgery. It is especially important for patients to be aware of what it will be like when they awaken from surgery as this decreases anxiety. It is also important for the patient's family to understand the amount and types of medical devices used in the intensive care unit (ICU). If allowed and time permits, patients and family members should be given a tour of the ICU. It is also important to teach patients and family the length of the usual stay in the ICU and what to expect during that time. Patients may be surprised to learn that they may be asked to get out of bed into a chair as early as the morning after surgery.

Pre-op teaching should also include presence of chest tubes and epicardial wires, early ambulation, need for pain medication, use of an incentive spirometer or other deep breathing exercises, and incision care. This helps mentally prepare the patient and family for post-op recovery.

▶ **NURSING IMPLICATIONS:** Educating patients and families about what to expect after surgery is an important nursing function. Nurses working in pre-op areas should familiarize themselves with the practices of their own institution so that accurate information is given and questions can be answered.

## ESSENTIAL FACTS

Patients who are adequately educated prior to surgery tend to have increased compliance post-op and may have an easier recovery from surgery. Involved family members and close friends can assist and should be included in education.

## Pre-Op Medications

Patients should understand the reasons for any medications given pre-op. It is especially important that patients who will be admitted from home on the day of surgery understand what medications they should take and what medications should be held prior to surgery. Since it is important to minimize ischemia prior to surgery, nitrates, beta-blockers, and statins are administered up to and including the day of surgery. Beta-blockers have been shown to reduce mortality and prevent atrial fibrillation and should be given within 24 hours of surgery unless the patient is severely bradycardic or hypotensive (Hillis et al., 2011). Clopidogrel (Plavix) and ticagrelor (Brilinta) should be held for at least 5 days, and prasugrel (Effient) should be held for at least 7 days prior to surgery

(Hillis et al., 2011). Patients who are taking one of these antiplatelet medications and undergo surgery have more blood loss and require more blood products during surgery. Patients who have elective surgery may be asked to hold aspirin for several days prior to surgery. However, patients experiencing acute coronary syndrome or ischemia should take aspirin up to and including the day of surgery. Oral hypoglycemics and long-acting insulin should generally be held on the day of surgery. Patients who no longer produce endogenous insulin (type 1 diabetics) must be provided with a basal insulin (long-acting insulin or insulin infusion) prior to and during surgery. Patients should be asked to stop taking herbal supplements several weeks prior to surgery.

▶ **NURSING IMPLICATIONS:** Nurses play a large role in helping patients understand what medications to take. Nurses should have a good understanding of medications and why they are administered so accurate education can take place. Nurses are also in the unique position to catch orders that may have been missed and question orders that are out of the ordinary.

## PREVENTION OF INFECTION

Post-op infection can be a very serious or fatal complication. Superficial wound infections have a mortality rate of 10% and deep sternal wound infections carry a mortality rate of 47% (Hillis et al., 2011). A number of steps should be taken to prevent infection. Patients are asked to shower with an antibacterial soap, such as chlorhexidine, on several occasions prior to surgery, usually the day before and the morning of surgery. Alternatively, wipes premoistened with chlorhexidine may be used. (If these are used, patients should be instructed to shower first, then apply the wipes without rinsing.) Patients on bed rest or who are unable to shower should receive several antibacterial scrubs administered by medical personnel.

Hair should be clipped from the chest and other areas where incisions are planned (chest from chin to groin, legs if veins will be harvested, forearms if radial arteries will be harvested). Clipping of hair is performed rather than shaving to prevent small nicks and cuts to the skin which may increase risk of infection (Hillis et al., 2011). Patients may be given an antibacterial mouth rinse containing chlorhexidine prior to surgery to reduce the bacterial count in the mouth. This may reduce the incidence of ventilator-associated pneumonia. In nasal carriers of *Staphylococcus aureus,* both methicillin-resistant and methicillin-sensitive, intranasal mupirocin may reduce the rate of nosocomial *S. aureus* infection (Hillis et al., 2011). Immediately prior to surgery (within 1 hour of the incision), patients are given one or more broad-spectrum antibiotics to further prevent infection. Antibiotics will be given at intervals for 24 to 48 hours post-op.

▶ **NURSING IMPLICATIONS:** It is important for patients to understand the risk of infection and the steps being taken to prevent it. Patients who complete their own antibacterial shower should receive clear instructions on why and how. If they will be showering at home prior to surgery, written instructions should be provided.

## ESSENTIAL FACTS

> Post-op infection can increase length of stay, cause pain and suffering, and even lead to death. Great care should be taken to prevent the occurrence of post-op infections.

## PATIENTS REQUIRING MORE INTENSIVE CARE PRIOR TO SURGERY

Sometimes patients with extensive disease or those in cardiogenic shock require care in an acute care unit or ICU prior to surgery. Patients with severe disease of the left main coronary artery, with very poor cardiac function, or with recent myocardial infarction causing cardiogenic shock may require placement of an intraaortic balloon pump (IABP) prior to surgery. Also, use of an IABP in high-risk patients (those undergoing repeat coronary artery bypass grafting, those with a left ventricular ejection fraction of less than 30%, or those with left main coronary artery disease) has been shown to reduce mortality (Hillis et al., 2011). IABP consists of placement of a large balloon into the aorta via the femoral artery. The balloon sits between the renal arteries and the arch of the aorta. The balloon inflates during diastole, pushing blood toward the heart as the balloon fills and displaces blood. This action pushes blood down the coronary arteries, increasing perfusion. The balloon deflates during systole, pulling blood from the left ventricle to fill the vacuum left by the balloon. This effectively decreases afterload and assists the left ventricle, allowing it to rest prior to surgery (Figure 3.1).

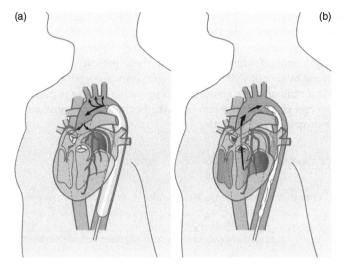

**FIGURE 3.1** Intraaortic balloon pump: (a) inflated, (b) deflated.

## ESSENTIAL FACTS

Patients requiring an IABP or vasopressors, or both, to support cardiac function and blood pressure prior to surgery are at much higher risk for surgical complications.

Patients with critical aortic stenosis in combination with coronary artery disease (CAD) are at high risk for sudden death and are usually kept in the hospital before surgery. It is important to monitor blood pressure in these patients. Because the aortic valve opening is so small, the left ventricle works hard to maintain cardiac output. If there is a decrease in left ventricular filling, cardiac output will fall. Because the aortic valve is a fixed diameter, the heart may not be able to compensate for the decrease in cardiac output. Thus, a fall in blood pressure may be fatal in these people. Caution should be taken when administering medications that may decrease systolic blood pressure below 90 mmHg. It may be wise to place these patients on bed rest to avoid orthostatic hypotension.

▶ **NURSING IMPLICATIONS:** Patients with critical aortic stenosis require careful monitoring to avoid hypotension. Caution should be taken when administering medications that may cause a drop in blood pressure. Dehydration should be avoided as this may lead to hypotension, and intravenous fluids should be ordered by a physician and administered while these patients are receiving nothing by mouth (NPO). Patients with critical aortic stenosis and CAD should never be allowed to get into a hot shower (e.g., to prep for surgery), as vasodilation from the hot water can cause an unsafe drop in blood pressure.

## ESSENTIAL FACTS

Whenever possible, patients should be prepared for surgery with adequate teaching and all appropriate tests. All possible steps should be taken to prevent infection and other post-op complications.

## REFERENCE

Hillis, L. D., Smith, P. K., Anderson, J. L., Bittl, J. A., Bridges C. R., Byrne J. G., . . . Winniford, M. D. (2011). 2011 ACCF/AHA guideline for coronary artery bypass graft surgery: A report of the American College of Cardiology Foundation/American Heart Association Task Force on Practice Guidelines. *Journal of the American College of Cardiology, 48,* e123–e210.

# Intraoperative Period

## Surgical Techniques

# 4

# Cardiopulmonary Bypass

*The first cardiac surgery was performed using cardiopulmonary bypass (CPB) in 1953. Since then, CPB has been used during thousands of surgeries and the technology has continued to evolve. Some cardiac surgeries are performed without CPB (off-pump), but the majority are performed using CPB. Even with current techniques, patients undergoing surgery using CPB face a number of potential complications. It is important to keep in mind the effect of CPB on the body and watch for these complications.*

## Objectives

In this chapter, you will learn:

1. The purpose of cardiopulmonary bypass during cardiac surgery
2. The effects of cardiopulmonary bypass on the patient
3. Potential complications related to cardiopulmonary bypass

## CBP MACHINE

A CPB machine consists of a series of chambers connected by synthetic tubing, similar to tubing used for intravenous fluids. This tubing is typically made with biocompatible material and may be coated with substances, such as heparin, to make it more biocompatible. Blood drains by means of gravity into a reservoir, then moves through a chamber where it is oxygenated. A roller pump or centrifugal pump is used to propel blood through the machine. Just before being returned to the body, the blood passes through a filter to remove any clots or particles. Blood may also be heated or cooled as it moves through the CPB machine, assisting in obtaining mild hypothermia or rewarming (Figure 4.1).

CPB is set up and managed by a perfusionist, who is specially trained to manage this therapy. Before placing a patient on CPB, the perfusionist primes the machine with a balanced electrolyte solution. It requires up to 2,000 mL of fluid to prime the machine, which results in hemodilution when the patient's blood mixes with the fluid. Often, the addition of albumin to the electrolyte solution is used to minimize the effects of hemodilution, but this will still result in a decrease in hematocrit. In some instances, the patient's own blood is used to displace the priming solution (called

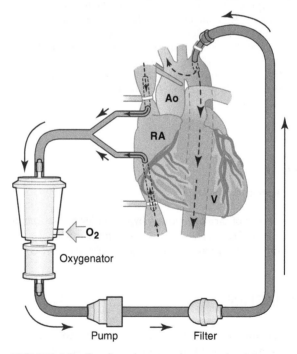

**FIGURE 4.1** Cardiopulmonary bypass circuit.
Ao, aorta; RA, right atrium; V, ventricle.

retrograde autologous priming) and virtually eliminate hemodilution. This can decrease the need for blood transfusions after surgery, but can cause problems with hypotension during surgery (Moorjani, Ohri, & Wechsler, 2014).

### ESSENTIAL FACTS

Patients placed on CPB generally experience hemodilution and a corresponding fall in hematocrit. This can be clinically significant, especially if the patient was anemic prior to surgery.

## INITIATION OF CBP

The patient is brought into the operating room. An arterial line and a pulmonary artery catheter are placed for hemodynamic monitoring. Anesthesia is induced and the patient is intubated. An incision must be made and the heart must be accessible for placing catheters prior to placing the patient on the CPB machine. The patient must be anticoagulated to prevent clot formation in the CPB circuit. Heparin is used most commonly for anticoagulation unless the patient has recently experienced heparin-induced thrombocytopenia (HIT), a type of heparin allergy. Heparin is administered until the activated clotting time (ACT) is 480 seconds or greater. The exact ACT required depends on the complexity of the surgery and preference of the surgeon.

### Catheter Placement

Once the patient is ready to be placed on CPB, a large catheter is inserted into the right atrium through an opening made in the right atrial appendage or wall of the right atrium. This is the venous catheter, which will drain blood via gravity into the CPB machine. Another catheter is placed into the ascending aorta. If the ascending aorta is calcified or for some other reason cannot be used, this catheter will be placed in the femoral or axillary artery. Blood is returned to the patient from the CPB machine through this arterial catheter.

Once the catheters are placed, the CPB machine slowly begins to remove blood from the patient. The patient's response is monitored and catheter placement checked. With the catheters in place and the CPB machine oxygenating the blood, the aorta is clamped to stop blood flow. At this point, the heart is stopped and the lungs deflated to perform the surgery.

## Cardioplegia

A concentrated electrolyte solution is infused into the heart to cause cardiac arrest (cardioplegia). This solution is infused either through a catheter placed in the aortic root (cardioplegia moves forward into the coronary arteries—called antegrade) or through a catheter in the coronary sinus (cardioplegia moves backward into the coronary veins—called retrograde). This infusion may be repeated multiple times during the surgery to ensure that the heart does not beat during the surgery.

Cardioplegia serves several functions. It keeps the heart muscle still to allow surgery to be more easily completed. It also greatly reduces the metabolic needs and oxygen requirements of the heart muscle, reducing the amount of ischemia during surgery.

## DURING BYPASS

While the patient's blood is being oxygenated via CPB, ventilations are stopped and the lungs are usually deflated. This expands the surgical field and allows the surgeon more access to the heart. During this time, oxygenation is controlled by the perfusionist. Adequate anticoagulation must be maintained throughout the period the patient is on CPB.

### Blood Pressure During CPB

CPB maintains a steady blood pressure; there is no systolic–diastolic pulsatile flow. The arterial line, used to measure blood pressure, registers a mean arterial pressure (MAP), not a systolic or diastolic pressure. During CPB, it is important to keep the MAP high enough to perfuse the brain, kidneys, and other organs. The perfusionist works with the anesthesiologist to keep this pressure between 60 and 80 mmHg. If the patient had preexisting renal insufficiency, the MAP during CPB will be kept closer to 80 mmHg. The kidneys are especially sensitive to low blood pressures and do not tolerate the nonpulsatile flow of CPB as well as other organs. Similarly, if the patient has known atherosclerosis of the carotid or cerebral arteries, the MAP will need to be kept higher to perfuse the brain during surgery.

## Coagulopathy

CPB can cause bleeding or clotting problems during and after surgery. Despite advances in making the tubing used for CPB more biocompatible, the blood still reacts to contact with this foreign substance. Platelets are activated, placing the patient at high risk for clotting. This is the reason anticoagulation is essential during CPB. As the blood mixes with the fluid used to prime the CPB machine, platelets and clotting factors are diluted. In addition, platelets may be destroyed as they move through the pumping mechanism of the CPB machine. This becomes important after surgery, when the patient is at high risk for bleeding.

## Systemic Inflammatory Response to CPB

When a patient's blood comes in contact with the components of the CPB machine, the complement system and several other pro-inflammatory pathways are activated. This produces a systemic inflammatory response, which typically lasts for several days after surgery. Mechanical trauma caused by the oxygenator can contribute to the inflammatory response. The endothelial lining of the arteries senses the inflammatory markers released by the complement system, leading to endothelial dysfunction.

In addition, factors related to the operative field and the CPB oxygenator can produce particulate emboli, consisting of red cell debris, platelet aggregates, fibrin, fat, and foreign material. The majority of large emboli (greater than 40 micrometers) are removed by the filter in the CPB circuit, but smaller emboli may obstruct capillaries and result in ischemic cell death. The combination of systemic inflammatory response and cell death results in increased capillary permeability (leaking capillaries), vasodilation (which can lower blood pressure and systemic vascular resistance), interstitial and peripheral edema, and organ dysfunction. In some patients, organ dysfunction is subclinical, but in patients with a larger inflammatory response or when there is less functional reserve, organ dysfunction may be clinically significant (Moorjani et al., 2014). The risk of damage to organs increases the longer the patient remains on CPB.

## ESSENTIAL FACTS

Deflation of the lungs during surgery results in atelectasis and pulmonary effusions post-op. Hypotension during surgery may result in ischemia and failure of various organs after surgery. Patients who have been on CPB often experience coagulopathies. This places them at high risk for bleeding after surgery. CPB causes a systemic inflammatory response, which may result in edema and organ damage.

## COMING OFF BYPASS

Before the heart is restarted, the surgeon carefully checks for and removes any air that might be in the heart chambers. The heart is restarted, using a temporary pacemaker via epicardial pacing wires, if necessary. Inotropes or vasopressors are given if needed so that the heart will support the cardiac output needs of the body. Once the patient is ready to be removed from CPB, flow from the CPB machine is gradually weaned and the catheters are removed. Repairs are then made to the areas where the catheters were placed.

### Reversing Anticoagulation

At the end of the surgery, just before the CPB catheters are removed, anticoagulation is reversed using protamine sulfate. Protamine reverses the effect of heparin by binding to the heparin molecule and making it ineffective. Heparin lasts longer than protamine in the blood, so rebound anticoagulation may be seen.

If protamine sulfate is given too rapidly, severe hypotension may occur. Also, in some rare instances, a patient may have a reaction to protamine. This may be demonstrated by increased pulmonary artery pressures, hypotension, and anaphylaxis. Patients at risk of experiencing anaphylaxis are those who have previously undergone cardiopulmonary bypass, diabetics who have received insulin with protamine (NPH insulin), patients who are allergic to fish (protamine is made from fish sperm), and men who have undergone vasectomy or are infertile (may have antibodies to protamine). Patients who receive repeated doses of protamine are also at risk. Patients who experience a reaction to protamine sulfate should be treated symptomatically and should not receive future doses.

## *ESSENTIAL FACTS*

After surgery, patients should be monitored for a protamine reaction. This potentially life-threatening complication may be less severe if recognized and treated promptly.

## *ESSENTIAL FACTS*

Despite efforts to decrease the negative effects of CPB, it has the potential to cause ischemia to various organs and usually induces an inflammatory response. The risk of damage to organs increases the longer the patient is on CPB.

## REFERENCE

Moorjani, N., Ohri, S. K., & Wechsler, A. S. (2014). *Cardiac surgery: Recent advances and techniques.* Boca Raton, FL: CRC Press.

# 5

# Coronary Artery Bypass Graft Surgery

As catheter-based technologies, such as angioplasty and stenting, continue to improve, more patients are being treated in the cardiac cath lab instead of being sent for cardiac surgery. Some patients may be treated repeatedly using interventional techniques, and cardiac surgery may be delayed for years. However, coronary artery bypass grafting (CABG) surgery remains the mainstay of treatment for coronary artery disease. Patients undergo CABG to decrease anginal symptoms and improve survival.

## Objectives

In this chapter, you will learn:

1. How the heart is accessed during CABG surgery
2. What bypass conduits may be used and how they are harvested
3. Surgical techniques that may lead to potential complications after surgery

## ACCESSING THE HEART

To access the heart, the surgeon makes an incision down the middle of the chest (midline sternotomy). The sternum itself must be cut using a saw, and retractors are used to spread the chest open to visualize the chest cavity. As described in Chapter 4, the patient is placed on cardiopulmonary bypass, and the heart is stopped using a concentrated electrolyte (cardioplegia) solution. The lungs are deflated in most cases to allow more room for the surgeon to work.

## THE BYPASS CONDUITS

A vessel chosen as a bypass conduit needs to meet certain criteria. Removing it from the body should not impair circulation, it should be long enough to reach from the aorta to the coronary artery, and it must be the right size to attach to a coronary artery. The greater saphenous vein has been the traditional choice of conduit for CABG surgery. An artery used as a conduit has the advantage of lasting longer without reocclusion than a saphenous vein. The two most commonly used arteries are the internal mammary artery (IMA) and the radial artery.

### Saphenous Vein

The saphenous vein is usually harvested endoscopically (using a small camera inserted into small incisions) or using a skip incision (a series of small incisions separated by intact skin). This is chosen over an open harvest to decrease pain, decrease leg edema, and speed wound healing. However, patients for whom these techniques are not possible will have their vein harvested using an open incision. The saphenous vein, like all veins, has valves that serve to keep blood flowing toward the heart. When a saphenous vein is used as a bypass conduit, the valves must be removed or it must be turned backward so that they do not obstruct the flow of blood in the bypass graft. When using a saphenous vein graft (SVG), the surgeon sews one end to the aorta and the other end to a coronary artery distal to the occlusion.

### Internal Mammary Artery

The IMAs run from the subclavian artery to the right and left sides of the chest wall. Either IMA makes for a long-lasting bypass graft. The left internal mammary artery (LIMA) is most commonly used

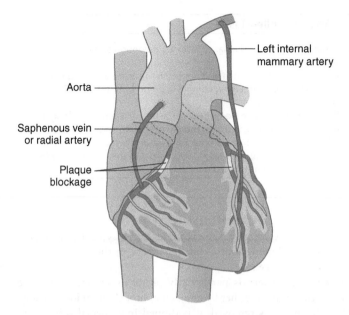

**FIGURE 5.1** Bypass grafts. The saphenous vein or radial artery graft in this drawing is sewn proximally into the aorta and distally into the right coronary artery (RCA) below the occlusion. The left internal mammary artery (LIMA) in this drawing remains attached to the subclavian artery at the proximal end and the distal end is sewn into the left anterior descending artery (LAD).

to bypass occlusions in the left anterior descending artery (LAD). The right internal mammary artery (RIMA) may be used to bypass occlusions in the right coronary artery (RCA). To use an IMA, the surgeon carefully dissects the distal end of the artery away from the chest wall and sews it into a coronary artery beyond the occlusion (Figure 5.1). There is minimal manipulation of the artery, so chances of spasm are minimized.

## Radial Artery

The radial artery is harvested from either the right or left wrist. Before removing the artery, an Allen test is performed to make sure the ulnar artery is patent and will perfuse the hand with blood (Table 5.1). If it is determined that blood flow to the hand

| TABLE 5.1  Allen Test |
| --- |

1. Locate the radial and ulnar arteries by palpation and compress both simultaneously
2. Ask the patient to clench and unclench the corresponding hand 10 times while maintaining compression on both arteries. The hand should look very pale
3. Release compression from the ulnar artery and time how long it takes for flushing to return to the palm, thumb, and nail beds
4. If it takes longer than 6 seconds for flushing to return to the hand, flow through the ulnar artery is impaired and the radial artery from this hand should not be used as a bypass graft

will be inadequate if the radial artery is removed, another bypass conduit will be sought. The radial artery is typically harvested from the nondominant arm, but the artery in the dominant arm may be used if needed.

The radial artery is particularly prone to spasm. It must be harvested carefully, either by an open approach or endoscopically. After the artery is removed, it is dipped in a special solution to reduce spasm. Then, one end is sewn to the aorta and the other is sewn to a coronary artery below the occlusion (see Figure 5.1). To prevent spasm of the radial graft, an intravenous solution of either nitroglycerin (Tridil) or diltiazem (Cardizem) is started. This is continued until the patient can take an oral antispasmotic medication. The oral medication is continued for several months until the risk of spasm of the radial artery graft has passed.

## ESSENTIAL FACTS

Removing the saphenous vein makes the patient more prone to lower extremity edema, which can delay wound healing and increase the risk of infection. Using an IMA as a bypass graft increases the risk of sternal infection, especially in patients with other risk factors and if both the right and left IMAs are used. If a radial artery is used as a bypass graft, either oral nitroglycerin (Isordil) or diltiazem (Cardizem) is typically given for a few months to decrease the risk of spasm in the graft.

## Surgical Markers

Some surgeons place metal clips or rings in the chest to mark the location of bypass grafts. If the patient returns in the future with chest pain, these markers, visible radiographically, can assist the cardiologist in the cath lab in finding the grafts in order to inject dye and determine patency.

## CLOSING THE CHEST

Once the bypass grafts have been placed, the surgeon places chest tubes in the mediastinal and pleural spaces to drain any blood or fluid that may accumulate. Epicardial pacing wires are attached to the surface of the heart. Usually several pacing wires are attached to the anterior surface of the heart near the atrium and near the ventricle. The other end of the pacing wires is needle-like and is pushed through the chest wall and connected to a temporary pacemaker. The lungs must be reinflated, the heart restarted, and hemodynamic stability achieved before the chest can be closed. The retractors are removed and the sternum is sewn together with wire. Sternal wires give stability until the bone heals. Once the sternum is securely wired together, the other tissue layers are closed. Sterile dressings are placed over all incisions and the patient is prepared to move to the intensive care unit.

### ESSENTIAL FACTS

It is important to know which grafts were used during surgery, as it may change the plan of care for patients after surgery. If SVGs were used, pain and edema in the affected leg may be an issue. If a radial graft was used, the patient must be given medications post-op to prevent spasm of the artery.

# 6

# Valve Surgery

*The function of the four heart valves is to maintain the forward flow of blood in the body. Each valve needs to open wide enough to allow blood to quickly flow through and close tight enough to prevent blood from flowing backward. When one or more valves fail to perform one of these functions, it has serious implications to the patient (see Chapter 1). Many patients undergo surgery to repair or replace heart valves. This surgery may be the only treatment performed (isolated valve surgery) or be done in combination with coronary artery bypass grafting (see Chapter 5) or other therapies (see Chapter 7). Many times, these patients have more comorbidities than patients who have surgery to treat coronary artery disease alone.*

## Objectives

In this chapter, you will learn:

1. Factors that influence the choice of tissue or mechanical valve
2. Why some valves are repaired and some are replaced
3. Postoperative implications of valve surgery

## VALVE SURGERY

Valve surgery is truly an open heart surgery. Not only must the chest be opened and the heart accessed (see Chapter 5), but the surgeon must cut into the heart tissue itself to work on the valves. These surgeries are longer and more complicated that an isolated coronary artery bypass graft surgery, putting the patient at higher risk of complications. Because the atrial tissue is opened to access the valves, patients who undergo valve surgery are at much higher risk of developing atrial fibrillation post-op. They may also have myocardial edema post-op, which will prolong recovery time.

## TISSUE VERSUS MECHANICAL VALVE

The choice of a tissue or mechanical valve is one made prior to surgery, when possible. This is a decision made between the surgeon and the patient and depends on a number of factors. The patient's preference, age, lifestyle, occupation, and recreational activities should be taken into account when making the decision.

### Tissue Valve

Tissue valves may be made from porcine (pork), bovine (cow), or human (homograft) tissue. Most of the tissue valves implanted are porcine or bovine, often with some manufactured component in addition to the tissue. Tissue valves are desirable for many patients because they do not require anticoagulation and are ideal for patients for whom anticoagulation is contraindicated. Traditionally, tissue valves have not been as durable as mechanical valves, so they have not been the best option for younger patients. However, advances in technology have produced tissue valves that can last up to 20 years.

### Mechanical Valves

Mechanical valves are composed entirely of manufactured materials, such as metal alloys, carbon-based materials, and Dacron. There are several different types of mechanical valves. Because mechanical valves are long-lasting, they may be a good option for younger patients requiring valve replacement. However, mechanical valves are prone to clot formation, so patients will require anticoagulation as long as the valve is in place. This makes them a poor choice for the elderly, patients who cannot tolerate anticoagulation, and recipients who engage in activities (sports, occupations) that place them at high risk for trauma.

*ESSENTIAL FACTS*

Tissue valves do not require anticoagulation but may not last as long as mechanical valves. Mechanical valves are very durable, but require life-long anticoagulation to prevent clot formation on the valve.

## VALVE REPLACEMENT OR REPAIR

Patients who require valve surgery may undergo valve repair or valve replacement. Whenever possible, it is preferable to repair the patient's own valve instead of replacing the valve. This provides a longer-lasting valve with fewer complications. Replacing the valve is more complicated and may involve correctly sizing and sewing in the new valve and reattaching or repairing cordae tendonae. The option to repair or replace a valve depends on the valve in question and the extent and type of disease affecting the valve.

### Aortic Stenosis

Patients with aortic stenosis require valve replacement with either a tissue or mechanical valve. A stenotic aortic valve cannot be repaired. Aortic valve replacement is made more difficult because the coronary arteries originate from the aorta directly above the aortic valve. The surgeon must take great care that the coronary arteries are not disturbed during the surgery or must move them to a better location on the aorta.

Some patients younger than 50 years of age with aortic stenosis may undergo a Ross procedure. This involves removing the aortic valve, placing the patient's own pulmonic valve in the aortic position, and replacing the pulmonic valve with a homograft (human tissue valve). This is possible because both the aortic and pulmonic valves are tricuspid valves (Figure 6.1). This procedure uses the patient's own, healthy valve in place of the stenotic aortic valve, providing durability. And, since the pulmonic valve is

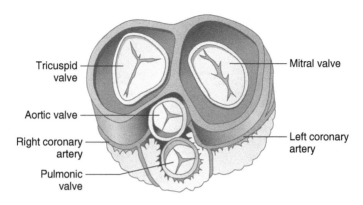

**FIGURE 6.1** Appearance and configuration of the valves.

under much lower pressures than the aortic valve, a homograft in place of the pulmonic valve will last a long time. This is a long, complicated surgery, but is a longer-term solution than replacing the aortic valve with a tissue valve and avoids the anticoagulation necessary when replacing the aortic valve with a mechanical valve.

## Aortic Insufficiency

Patients with aortic insufficiency have the same options for replacement as those with aortic stenosis. Patients with endocarditis in the aortic valve benefit from a homograft (human tissue valve), which has less risk of developing endocarditis in the new valve. In addition, an insufficient aortic valve may sometimes be repaired. If the aortic insufficiency is accompanied by aortic aneurysm (widening of the aorta), the valve and diseased portion of the aorta may be replaced with a valve connected to a sleeve-like conduit. This conduit is used to replace the enlarged portion of the aorta. The surgeon will need to implant the coronary arteries into the conduit once it is in place (Figure 6.2).

## *ESSENTIAL FACTS*

Aortic stenosis cannot be repaired and the valve must be replaced. In aortic insufficiency, the valve may be repaired or replaced.

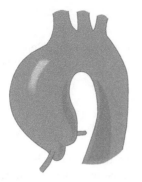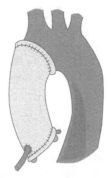

**FIGURE 6.2** Replacement of the aortic valve and proximal portion of the aorta.

## Mitral Stenosis

In mitral stenosis, if the valve leaflets are calcified or fibrotic, the valve must be replaced with either a tissue or mechanical valve. In some cases, the leaflets are still functional but have become fused together. The area where the valve leaflets touch when closed is called a commissure. Sometimes, scar tissue develops along this line, preventing the leaflets from opening. If this is the case, the valve may be repaired by cutting along this line and allowing the leaflets to open. This procedure is called a commissurotomy.

## Mitral Regurgitation

In mitral regurgitation, repair is possible in 90% of cases and is the treatment of choice. If the regurgitation results from dilation of the valve that prevents the leaflets from closing, a stiff ring, called an annuloplasty ring, may be sewn in around the valve opening to shore up the valve and make the opening smaller. Sometimes, this alone is enough to repair the regurgitation. If the valve leaflets are enlarged or damaged, the leaflets can also be repaired. A small piece of one of the leaflets may be removed to allow the leaflet to close properly. Chordae tendinae may be replaced or moved to a better location to improve the function of the valve. Sometimes a combination of these techniques is used to repair the valve. If it is not possible to repair the regurgitant valve, the mitral valve will be replaced with either a tissue or a mechanical valve.

## ESSENTIAL FACTS

A mitral valve will be repaired whenever possible. Repair is possible in 90% of cases of mitral regurgitation and in some cases of mitral stenosis.

## Tricuspid Valve

Tricuspid stenosis is rare. In these cases, the valve may be repaired by commissurotomy or replaced with a tissue or mechanical valve. Tricuspid regurgitation sometimes occurs as a result of disease in the mitral valve. This association is multifactorial, but may be caused by increases in left atrial pressure as a result of mitral valve disease. This pressure in turn may cause pulmonary hypertension, which causes the right ventricle to work harder to push blood to the lungs. This increase in work causes hypertrophy in the usually thin-walled right ventricle. This expands the tricuspid valve annulus (diameter) and leads to regurgitation (Shiran & Sagie, 2009).

The AV node and the bundle of His run directly next to the tricuspid valve. The surgeon must be very careful not to disturb these parts of the conduction system. Patients who undergo repair or replacement of the tricuspid valve are prone to heart blocks and new bundle branch blocks after surgery.

## ESSENTIAL FACTS

Nurses should know what valve was affected and if it was repaired or replaced. Patient care implications include educating the patient about the procedure, watching for atrial fibrillation and other arrhythmias (especially heart blocks), and anticoagulation for patients undergoing replacement with mechanical valves.

## REFERENCE

Shiran, A. & Sagie, A. (2009). Tricuspid regurgitation in mitral valve disease: Incidence, prognostic implications, mechanism, and management. *Journal of the American College of Cardiology, 53,* 401–408.

# 7

# Other Surgical Treatments

*In addition to coronary artery bypass grafting (CABG) surgery and valve surgery, various surgical treatments may be performed by cardiovascular surgeons. They may be performed alone or in combination with other procedures. The goal with all of these surgeries is to decrease the number and severity of complications after heart surgery and improve quality of life.*

## Objectives

In this chapter, you will learn:

1. Treatments for atrial fibrillation that are performed in the operating room
2. When a patient might benefit from transmyocardial revascularization
3. When a ventricular assist device might be used in a patient

## TREATMENT OF ATRIAL FIBRILLATION

### Atrial Fibrillation

Many patients with valve disease develop atrial fibrillation before surgical intervention due to stretching and irritation of atrial tissue. Many other patients without preexisting atrial fibrillation develop this complication after surgery due to irritation, inflammation, or edema of the atria resulting from surgery. This is especially true for patients who undergo mitral valve surgery.

Atrial fibrillation is the result of chaotic electrical activity and disorganized depolarization in the atria. Atrial fibrillation may be classified as paroxysmal (starts and stops spontaneously within 7 days), persistent (fails to convert within 7 days; can be converted to sinus rhythm with medications or cardioversion), or permanent (present for more than a year; cardioversion has not been attempted or has failed). Paroxysmal atrial fibrillation may recur over and over with varying frequency.

While a patient is in atrial fibrillation, the atria do not contract to eject blood into the ventricles (known as atrial kick), so ventricular filling is completely due to passive atrial emptying. Due to the loss of atrial kick, the ventricle loses some stretch of muscle fibers, which causes the force of contraction of the ventricle to be smaller, leading to a decrease in cardiac output. This decrease in cardiac output can be especially detrimental to patients who have recently undergone surgery. In addition, atrial fibrillation puts patients at risk of stroke, since blood is stagnant and clots may form in the atria. These clots may break loose, embolize to the vessels in the brain, and cause a stroke. In addition, both the right and left atria have a pouch, called an atrial appendage, where clots are especially prone to form.

## ESSENTIAL FACTS

Atrial fibrillation may occur before or after cardiac surgery and is a common but serious complication of cardiac surgery. It also increases the risk of stroke.

Atrial fibrillation is often difficult to treat. One treatment for atrial fibrillation is to limit the chaotic electrical activity by creating lines of nonconductive tissue through the atria. Creating these lines around the pulmonary veins has been found to be effective in treating atrial fibrillation in many people. This can be done via ablation or a maze procedure.

# Ablation

Ablation refers to the destruction of myocardial tissue in a particular place. Areas of dead tissue heal and form scar tissue, which does not conduct electrical current. There are several methods of creating these lines of dead tissue. Radiofrequency ablation uses radio waves to heat tissue in a localized area to the point that the myocardial cells die. Cryoablation uses extreme cold to freeze cells to the point that they expand and die. Either way, lines of dead tissue are formed that will become scar tissue and prevent the spread of electrical activity beyond these lines. Either radiofrequency ablation or cryoablation may be done during surgery while the chest is open or during a minimally invasive procedure (see Chapter 8).

For patients with paroxysmal atrial fibrillation, using ablation to surround and isolate the pulmonary veins is an effective treatment 90% of the time. For patients with persistent or permanent atrial fibrillation, a maze procedure has the best success rate.

# Maze Procedure

The maze procedure is most commonly performed as an adjunct to mitral valve surgeries. Patients with mitral valve disease are particularly prone to atrial fibrillation both before and after mitral valve surgery. During the maze procedure, the surgeon cuts along specified lines in the atrium and then sews the cut areas closed. As the tissue heals, scar tissue forms, which prevents propagation of electrical activity beyond these lines. The maze procedure creates lines of scar tissue that electrically isolate the pulmonary veins, located in the left atrium (Figure 7.1). Sometimes lines are also cut in the right atrium.

## ESSENTIAL FACTS

Both ablation and a maze procedure create lines of scar tissue through the atria, usually focusing on isolating the pulmonary veins. These lines prevent the chaotic spread of electrical activity that characterizes atrial fibrillation.

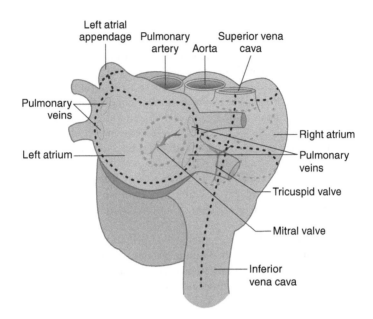

**FIGURE 7.1** Lines cut in the atria during a maze procedure to stop the propagation of chaotic electrical activity associated with atrial fibrillation.

## Removal of the Atrial Appendage

When a patient is in atrial fibrillation, clots frequently form in the atrial appendages. Clots in the left atrial appendage can embolize and cause stroke. A way to reduce the risk of stroke in patients with atrial fibrillation is to surgically remove the left atrial appendage. This is frequently done in conjunction with a maze procedure. The right atrial appendage is sometimes removed as well.

## TRANSMYOCARDIAL REVASCULARIZATION

It is not always possible to revascularize (return blood flow to) every area of the heart. In addition, not every patient who needs additional blood flow to the heart is able to undergo the stresses of surgery. There are not many options to restore blood flow and reduce symptoms for these patients. One possible option is transmyocardial revascularization (TMR), which may be done as an adjunct to CABG surgery or through a small thoracotomy incision. TMR involves using a laser or $CO_2$ to drill holes into the myocardial tissue in the area that cannot be revascularized. These holes will soon close, but the resulting inflammatory response stimulates the growth of new vessels (called angiogenesis).

### ESSENTIAL FACTS

TMR may be performed in patients who have no other options for restoring blood flow to ischemic areas of the heart.

## VENTRICULAR AND CIRCULATORY ASSIST DEVICES

Patients in acute heart failure or cardiogenic shock may need additional mechanical support for blood circulation in the body. In addition, some patients have very poor ventricular function, and the surgeon may have a difficult time weaning them off cardiopulmonary bypass. In these instances, percutaneous circulatory devices may be used to support the patient until the heart recovers enough to pump an adequate amount of blood to the body.

An intraaortic balloon pump (IABP) may help support the patient's cardiac output enough to wean off bypass or in the short term after surgery (see Chapter 3). IABP is a low-cost device and is easy to implant. It is the only form of mechanical assistance available in many intensive care units. The most common complication of IABP is leg ischemia (Westaby, 2014).

### Left Ventricular Assist

Left ventricular assist devices (LVADs) provide perfusion to the body while decompressing (reducing volume in) the left ventricle. This decompression reduces the strain and oxygen demand of the left ventricle. For an LVAD to function, it must receive adequate volume (preload). Thus, there must be adequate intravascular volume and the right ventricle must be functioning well. When an LVAD is inserted, a catheter is placed in the left atrium to drain blood into a pumping device. This blood is returned to the aorta with enough pressure to perfuse the body.

When possible, inotropes should be weaned off to decrease myocardial oxygen demand. However, some patients develop a type of shock due to vasodilation and require vasopressin to maintain systemic blood pressures. In addition, most devices require anticoagulation to prevent clot formation in the pump or tubing. For these devices, the activated clotting time should be kept between 175 and 200 seconds, higher if the flow rate is transiently decreased. After 48 hours of LVAD support, the functioning of the left ventricle with minimal support may be assessed using transesophageal echocardiography (TEE). If the left ventricle is improving, the LVAD support may be weaned down until the patient is ready for removal of the device.

## Right Ventricular Assist

Patients with right ventricular failure may need support for the right ventricle. This can happen in isolation, but more commonly occurs with left ventricular failure. Right ventricular failure may become more evident after an LVAD is placed. There are several devices designed to support the right ventricle. They are implanted with a drainage catheter in the right atrium and a blood return catheter in the pulmonary artery. For the device to function correctly, the patient must have adequate intravascular volume and left ventricular function.

If the failure of the right ventricle is related to pulmonary hypertension, inhaled nitric oxide or prostacyclin may be used to reduce pulmonary artery pressures and improve functioning of the right ventricular assist device (RVAD) or assist with weaning from the device. The requirement for anticoagulation and the assessment for weaning are similar to those for an LVAD.

## Biventricular Assist

After cardiac surgery, a small number of patients require assist to both the left and right ventricles. A biventricular assist device (BiVAD) supports both pulmonary and systemic circulation. BiVAD support incorporates the techniques used for both LVAD and RVAD support. The need for anticoagulation and techniques for assessing improvement of functioning and ability to wean are similar to those described for LVADs. Overall survival is much reduced in patients requiring BiVAD support.

The Tandem Heart ventricular assist device involves placing a catheter in a femoral vein and threading it up into the right atrium. The catheter is then threaded through the septum into the left atrium. Blood is removed from the left atrium and returned to the body through another catheter in a femoral artery at a rate of 4 L/min. This decompresses the left ventricle and improves both blood pressure and cardiac output. Support of the right ventricle is possible by threading a catheter into the right atrium via a jugular vein and also into the pulmonary artery via a femoral vein. In one report of Tandem Heart use describing 117 patients, the mean cardiac index increased from 0.5 L/min/m$^2$ to 3 L/min/m$^2$ and systolic blood pressure increased from 75 to 100 mmHg. Complications included gastrointestinal bleeding, leg ischemia, and stroke. Displacement of the inflow cannula across the atrial septum back into the right atrium occurred on several occasions, causing profound desaturation and could be fatal within minutes if not corrected (Westaby, 2014).

The Impella device is inserted via the femoral artery, threaded over the aortic arch, and passed through the aortic valve into the left ventricle. It provides a flow of 2.5 L/min by removing blood from the left ventricle and pumping it into the aorta. The Impella may be left in place for up to a week. A larger version delivers up to 5 L/min but must be inserted surgically either using sternotomy or cutdown in the femoral or axillary artery. Limitations of this device include insufficient flow in larger patients, short duration of use, and potential for displacement out of the left ventricle. It is contraindicated in patients with aortic regurgitation or stenosis, and in those with a mechanical aortic valve. As with the other devices, there is a risk of leg ischemia (Westaby, 2014).

## Long-Term Assist

There have been many advances in circulatory support device technology, and several devices are now available to provide long-term support. These long-term devices are used for patients in whom recovery of heart functioning is not anticipated and in those who are potential candidates for heart transplant. Some devices have also been used as treatment for patients who are not candidates for heart transplant. When used in this manner, the treatment is called destination therapy. Most long-term devices are designed to

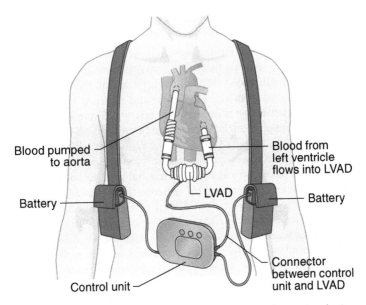

**FIGURE 7.2** Long-term implanted left ventricular assist device (LVAD).

support the circulatory function of the heart and will assist the left ventricle, the right ventricle, or both (Figure 7.2).

Long-term implanted LVADs consist of a pump, implanted in the patient's chest cavity with catheters going to and from the heart; a drive line, which exits the patient's chest wall; and several battery packs that are worn to power the device. Pumps may be pulsatile or continuous. Continuous pumps are smaller and more durable, but a pulse will not be palpable in patients who have a continuous pump. Extensive patient education must be provided on topics including infection prevention, battery use and battery life, and signs and symptoms to watch for.

## ESSENTIAL FACTS

Patients whose hearts are not able to support circulation or who are unable to be weaned off cardiopulmonary bypass (CPB) may benefit from a ventricular assist device. Patients may need support for the left ventricle, right ventricle, or both (biventricular).

Extracorporeal membrane oxygenation (ECMO) can sometimes serve as an alternative to ventricular assist devices. ECMO is also used when a patient's lungs are not able to oxygenate the blood, such as in severe pulmonary edema or acute respiratory distress syndrome (ARDS). In addition to assisting the pumping function of the heart, ECMO replaces the lungs in oxygenating the blood. ECMO consists of a membrane oxygenator, centrifugal pump, heat exchanger, and heparin-coated circuit, very similar to a CPB machine. If the need for ECMO is discovered soon enough during cardiac surgery, the same catheters used for CPB may also be used for ECMO (see Chapter 4). If the catheters used for CPB have been removed, one catheter may be placed in the internal jugular vein or femoral vein for venous drainage, and another in the carotid artery or femoral artery to return oxygenated blood to the body. Since ECMO provides nonpulsatile flow, an IABP is often inserted to assist with coronary perfusion.

While a patient is on ECMO, it is important to maintain adequate preload and treat pulmonary hypertension with nitrous oxide to allow for adequate blood flow. Anticoagulation should be avoided in these patients. The heparin-coated circuit prevents thrombus formation in the system. ECMO is designed for use for a few days. If there is no improvement after 2 days and the patient has suffered neurological damage, ECMO is often discontinued. If there is improvement in organ function within 5 days, the patient may be weaned off ECMO or transitioned to a longer term ventricular support device.

Patients who had multiorgan failure before the initiation of ECMO or who develop renal failure and the need for dialysis while on ECMO have a very high mortality rate. Of patients who receive ECMO due to cardiogenic shock following cardiac surgery, 40% to 50% will die on ECMO. Even though the rest may be weaned from ECMO, only about half of those will survive to hospital discharge.

## *ESSENTIAL FACTS*

ECMO may be used to oxygenate the blood as well as provide assistance for the pumping function of the heart. Mortality rates for these patients are very high.

# REFERENCE

Westaby, S. (2014). Mechanical circulatory support. In N. Moorjani, S. K. Ohri, & A. Wechsler (Eds.), *Cardiac surgery: Recent advances and techniques.*In , Boca Raton, FL: CRC Press.

# BIBLIOGRAPHY

Bojar, R. M. (2011). *Manual of perioperative care in adult cardiac surgery* (5th ed.). West Sussex, UK: Wiley-Blackwell.

Hardin, S. R., & Kaplow, R. (Eds.). (2010). *Cardiac surgery essentials for critical care nursing.* Sudbury, MA: Jones & Bartlett.

Woods, S. L., Froelicher, E. S. S., Motzer, S. U., & Bridges, E. J. (Eds.). (2010). *Cardiac nursing* (6th ed.). Philadelphia, PA: Wolters Kluwer/ Lippincott Williams & Wilkins.

# 8

# Off-Pump Surgeries and Minimally Invasive Techniques

*Over the years, efforts have been made to reduce complications and improve the outcomes of cardiac surgery. There is also a push to reduce costs and decrease length of stay associated with cardiac surgery. In the mid-1990s, advances were made that allow surgeons to perform coronary artery bypass on a beating heart. Further advances in technology and surgical techniques allow surgeons to perform coronary artery bypass and valve surgeries without the use of a midline sternotomy, using endoscopic techniques, and with the assistance of robotic technologies.*

## Objectives

In this chapter, you will learn:

1. How cardiac surgeries are performed without cardiopulmonary bypass
2. Several technologies and robotic devices that surgeons use to perform minimally invasive surgeries
3. What complications may occur as a result of a minimally invasive surgery

## OFF-PUMP SURGERIES

Chapter 4 discusses the many complications associated with the use of cardiopulmonary bypass (CPB) during cardiac surgery.

In an effort to reduce these complications, surgical techniques were developed that allow surgeons to operate without the use of CPB while the heart is still beating. This is often called off-pump coronary artery bypass (OPCAB). This method can only be used to operate on the surface of the heart; it cannot be used for patients who require valve surgery or any other surgery that requires cutting into the heart.

Either the use of strategically placed sutures or special positioning devices allows the surgeon to turn and position the heart to gain access to the surgical site. Bypass grafts are implanted in the manner discussed in Chapter 5. The one additional requirement is that the surgical site be held as still as possible. As the surgeon is sewing the graft to the coronary artery, a stabilization device must be used to hold that area still while the rest of the heart continues to beat. Stabilization devices are available that use either suction or pressure to hold this area still without damaging the heart muscle. Even with stabilization, this technique is more difficult than operating when the heart is still (cardiopulmonary standstill).

When OPCAB is performed, a perfusionist is on standby with a CPB machine. If there is bleeding that cannot be controlled, arrhythmias or ischemia that cannot be readily managed, or hemodynamic compromise when the heart is positioned, the patient will need to be placed on CPB and the heart stopped to complete the surgery.

Several studies have shown a decrease in mortality and need for blood transfusions with the use of OPCAB. Because CPB is not used, this technique may also decrease neurocognitive dysfunction, renal dysfunction, and atrial fibrillation. OPCAB may be performed using a midline sternotomy or may be combined with other minimally invasive techniques. Many surgeons no longer perform OPCAB unless combining the technique with a minimally invasive surgery. Others reserve this technique for patients with minimal coronary artery disease or for very high-risk patients for whom CPB needs to be avoided.

## ESSENTIAL FACTS

By avoiding CPB and operating on a beating heart, some of the complications associated with coronary artery bypass grafting (CABG) may be avoided.

A number of techniques and technologies allow for cardiac surgery to be performed in a minimally invasive manner. Generally, "minimally invasive" refers to surgery without the traditional midline sternotomy. The goals of a minimally invasive surgery include the following:

- Create patent grafts at least as well as traditional coronary bypass surgery
- Have the patient return to baseline activity faster
- Decrease length of stay and cost of the surgery
- Decrease morbidity, mortality, and pain

Minimally invasive surgeries have been shown to meet some of these goals. In general, minimally invasive cardiac surgery decreases the need for blood transfusions, length of stay, and risk of infection. Patients also experience a faster recovery time. However, other complications of cardiac surgery may or may not be decreased by the use of minimally invasive techniques.

Patient selection for minimally invasive cardiac surgery is important. Smaller incisions may impede full access to the heart. In general, patients must have disease in noncalcified arteries on the front of the heart (left anterior descending artery [LAD] or right coronary artery [RCA]). The arteries that will have bypass grafts sewn in must not be too small (i.e., must be greater than 1.5 mm in diameter) and generally there should be only one or two blockages to bypass. If the diseased artery is intramyocardial (deep in the cardiac muscle instead of on the surface), minimally invasive surgery is not possible. Many surgeons will not use minimally invasive techniques on the morbidly obese due to the difficulty in performing surgery through a small incision in this population. Minimally invasive surgeries are especially beneficial in patients who meet the preceding criteria and who are at very high risk for complications during percutaneous coronary intervention and traditional cardiac surgery.

## ESSENTIAL FACTS

Minimally invasive cardiac surgery generally refers to surgery without the use of a midline sternotomy. This may or may not involve cardiac standstill and use of CPB. The goal is to decrease complications of surgery and improve recovery time.

# Minimally Invasive Direct Coronary Artery Bypass

One of the minimally invasive techniques that may be used is minimally invasive direct coronary artery bypass (MIDCAB). MIDCAB surgeries require a much smaller incision than traditional CABG and are performed off pump on a beating heart. This technique is used most frequently to bypass the LAD with the left internal mammary artery (LIMA). Less frequently, the RCA may be bypassed using the right internal mammary artery (RIMA) or a saphenous vein graft (SVG) may be used. A 5- to 12-cm incision is made on either side of the sternum (depending on which coronary artery is to be bypassed) and part of the costal cartilage is removed to expose the heart and to allow room for surgical instruments. Rib spreaders are used to spread and elevate the rib cage for maximal view and room to operate. The patient is intubated with a double-lumen endotracheal tube so that either the right or left lung may be deflated to make more room for the surgery. A stabilizer must be used to isolate and still the portion of the heart into which the graft will be sewn (Figure 8.1).

Advantages of MIDCAB include decreased pain, faster return to baseline activity, shorter length of stay, avoidance of CPB, and decreased infection rates. Disadvantages include limited patient eligibility, limited choice of vessels on which to operate, limited access to the surgical field, technical difficulty, and risk of incomplete revascularization. This technique requires an experienced surgeon with specialized training. Because of the difficulties of operating on a beating heart in such a limited surgical field, there

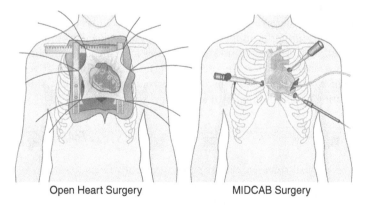

Open Heart Surgery                    MIDCAB Surgery

**FIGURE 8.1**  Traditional open heart surgery compared with minimally invasive direct coronary artery bypass (MIDCAB) surgery.

is increased risk of acute graft occlusion after surgery. In addition, this technique limits intervention to vessels on the front of the heart. Advances in technology have made percutaneous coronary intervention a more desirable option for many of these patients with limited disease.

*ESSENTIAL FACTS*

MIDCAB surgery involves a small incision without the use of CPB. However, few patients are eligible for this procedure and the surgery is technically difficult.

## Minimally Invasive Valve Surgery

The aortic valve or the mitral valve, or both, may be replaced or repaired without the use of a midline sternotomy. However, since the surgeon must cut into the heart to access the valves, CPB must be used and the heart must be stopped. To access the aortic valve, the surgeon makes a horizontal incision on the right side of the chest below the clavicle and above the nipple line. To access the mitral valve, the incision is made on the right side of the chest below the nipple line. In both cases, the costal cartilage is removed and rib spreaders are used to widen the surgical field as much as possible. Using a minimally invasive technique for valve surgery has been shown to decrease in-hospital mortality.

## Endoscopic Procedures

In recent years, technology for endoscopic procedures has advanced to the point that scopes are small enough and cameras have enough quality to perform cardiac surgeries. CABG and valve surgeries may be performed using endoscopic techniques. These surgeries typically involve the use of a thoracotomy incision and several small incisions that allow various instruments and cameras to be inserted. One or both lungs may be deflated to allow room to operate. CPB may be used during surgery so that the heart is still enough to work on. Owing to the use of endoscopic instruments and limited visibility, these surgeries require specialized training and are technically difficult to perform.

There are several technologies that allow for a minimally invasive maze procedure for patients with atrial fibrillation. An endoscopic maze procedure can be performed using a specialized ablation device. Sometimes called a mini-maze or extracardiac maze (ex-maze), this unique device allows for a maze procedure to be completed endoscopically on a beating heart. The traditional maze procedure (see Chapter 7), which involves cutting lines in the heart and sewing them up, cannot be performed on a beating heart. Stopping the heart requires the use of CPB, which comes with its own set of complications (see Chapter 4).

A minimally invasive ex-maze procedure involves the use of a small right thoracotomy incision. A midline incision is made below the sternum and through the diaphragm so that a camera can be inserted. The ablation catheter is also inserted through this incision to reach the back side of the heart. Two small incisions are made to either side of the midline incision for inserting surgical instruments. The right lung is deflated during this procedure to provide better access to the heart through the right thoracotomy incision. Once the heart is accessed and the ablation catheter is in place, the surgeon begins to create lines of nonconductive tissue across the atria using radiofrequency energy from the catheter. The lines are visible on the surface of the heart. These lines are made in the same areas as the lines created during the traditional cut-and-sew open maze procedure. (See Chapter 7 for more information about the maze procedure.) Since the heart is beating during this ablation procedure, the surgeon can tell the moment the patient converts from atrial fibrillation to normal sinus rhythm.

## ESSENTIAL FACTS

> Endoscopic cardiac surgeries involve the use of small incisions and specialized surgical instruments and cameras. One or both lungs may be deflated during surgery. The patient may be placed on CPB or the surgeon may perform a beating-heart surgery.

### Robotic-Assisted Surgeries

Recently, techniques have been developed that allow for the use of robotic devices to assist with minimally invasive cardiac surgeries. In a very similar manner to endoscopic procedures, surgical

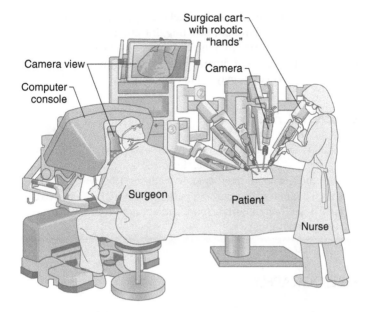

**FIGURE 8.2** Robotic surgery.

instruments and cameras are inserted into small incisions in the chest. The cardiac surgeon, instead of manipulating the instruments directly, sits at a computer console. The computer translates the surgeon's hand motions into motions of the surgical instruments. This allows for smaller instruments to be inserted and often involves more precise movements of the instruments. This technique allows for minimally invasive CABG and valve repair and replacement. However, the use of robotics for cardiac surgery is extremely expensive and requires extensive training for the surgical team (Figure 8.2).

## Complications of Minimally Invasive Cardiac Surgeries

The complications of cardiac surgery will be discussed in depth later in this book. Patients who have undergone minimally invasive or off-pump cardiac surgeries should be monitored for all potential complications of cardiac surgery. However, owing to the technically challenging nature of minimally invasive cardiac surgery, there are specific complications to watch for after these surgeries. These complications include dysrhythmias, hypotension, myocardial infarction, bleeding, infection, pulmonary complications, and injuries to bone and muscle at the surgical site. If blood flow is decreased during surgery, brain injury may occur. Rarely, lung herniation may occur after surgery.

## *ESSENTIAL FACTS*

Patients who undergo minimally invasive cardiac surgeries usually have fewer complications and a quicker recovery than those who undergo open procedures. However, serious complications still occur and patients need to be monitored closely for any potential complication after minimally invasive cardiac surgery.

## BIBLIOGRAPHY

Bojar, R. M. (2011). *Manual of perioperative care in adult cardiac surgery* (5th ed.). West Sussex, UK: Wiley-Blackwell.

Hardin, S. R., & Kaplow, R. (Eds.). (2010). *Cardiac surgery essentials for critical care nursing.* Sudbury, MA: Jones & Bartlett.

Kiser, A. C., & Cockfield, W. (2010). Paracardioscopic ex-maze procedure for atrial fibrillation. *Multimedia Manual of Cardiothoracic Surgery.* doi:10.1510/mmcts.2008.003863

Kiser, A. C., Wimmer-Greinecker, G., & Chitwood, W. R. (2007). Totally extracardiac maze procedure performed on the beating heart. *Annals of Thoracic Surgery, 84,* 1783–1785.

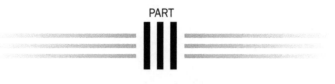

PART

III

# Initial Postoperative Period

# 9

# The First Few Hours: Initial Recovery

*The first few hours of recovery after cardiac surgery are critical and require skilled nursing care and attention. Patients are usually transferred to the intensive care unit (ICU) immediately after surgery for recovery from anesthesia and hemodynamic stabilization. The goals for this period are to stabilize the patient's hemodynamic status, maintain oxygenation, and normalize body temperature. Attaining these goals requires careful assessment and hemodynamic monitoring to quickly recognize and treat potential complications.*

*The nurse at the bedside has the responsibility to see the whole picture and work with the physician and other members of the health care team to optimize hemodynamic parameters. Managing medications and titrating vasoactive drips are critical steps to ensure cardiac output is maintained at an adequate level. The cardiac surgery nurse should know the actions of each ordered medication and when to use each. The nurse also must realize when treatments are not effective and notify the physician for further interventions.*

## Objectives

In this chapter, you will learn:

1. What assessments to perform during the initial post-op period
2. How to optimize cardiac output in the post-op cardiac surgery patient
3. How to assess for and manage potential complications of anesthesia

# PATIENT TRANSFER FROM OPERATING ROOM TO INTENSIVE CARE UNIT

Transferring the patient from the operating room to the ICU requires collaboration and communication among members of the health care team. The goal is to transfer the patient safely with all pertinent information communicated effectively.

## Hand-Off Communication

As a patient is being transferred from the operating room to the ICU, critical information must be relayed from the anesthesia provider to the receiving nurse. (See Table 9.1 for a list of information that should be relayed on transfer.) In addition, most patients would have had a pre-op assessment that can give information

**TABLE 9.1 Critical Information on Transfer From Operating Room to ICU**

| Pre-Op Information | Intra-Op Information | Post-Op Information |
|---|---|---|
| Patient medical and surgical history | Surgical procedure | Hemodynamic status |
| | Length of surgery | Ventilatory status |
| | Position on the operating room table | Current laboratory data |
| Pre-op status | Anesthetics and reversal agents used | Location and type of intravenous lines and catheters |
| | Intra-op complications | |
| | Cardiopulmonary bypass time | Type and rate of any vasopressors or inotropes |
| | Estimated blood loss | |
| | Type and amount of blood products and fluids given | Presence and location of pacing wires and chest tubes |
| | Anticoagulation given and reversal of anticoagulation | Presence and location of drains and dressings |
| | Any assistive devices used | |
| | Intake and output during surgery | |

about the risk of post-op complications. For example, a patient with preexisting pulmonary disease may have difficulty with weaning from the ventilator. Reviewing this pre-op assessment allows the nurse to anticipate and observe for potential complications in a patient-specific manner.

## ESSENTIAL FACTS

Knowledge of a patient's pre-op status, the surgical procedure performed, and any intraoperative complications assists the nurse in anticipating problems in the immediate post-op period.

## Initial Physical Assessment

Potential complications may be related to preexisting conditions and comorbidities of the patient, effects of anesthesia, or the surgical procedure itself. The initial physical assessment must be detailed and must include observation for potential complications. Specific complications commonly seen in the immediate post-op period will be discussed in Chapter 10. The following items should be a part of the initial physical assessment performed by the cardiac surgery nurse.

### Vital Signs and Hemodynamics

The patient's heart rate and rhythm, blood pressure, temperature, and pulse oximetry should be evaluated. Hemodynamic parameters should be measured, including pulmonary artery pressure, pulmonary artery occlusion pressure (PAOP; wedge pressure), central venous pressure (CVP), cardiac output, cardiac index (CI), and systemic vascular resistance (SVR). For some patients a mixed venous saturation is warranted. If so, this would be ordered by the physician and sent to the lab or performed on a bedside blood gas analyzer. Normal hemodynamic values for a post-op cardiac surgery patient are listed in Table 9.2; however, different values may be stated by the surgeon as acceptable for particular patients depending on their disease process and underlying comorbidities.

### Cardiac Assessment

A post-op baseline 12-lead electrocardiogram (ECG) should be performed to evaluate for ischemia and any conduction problems.

**TABLE 9.2 Normal Values of Hemodynamic Measurements for Post-Op Cardiac Surgery Patients**

| Measurement | Normal Values |
| --- | --- |
| Systolic blood pressure (SBP) | 100–130 mmHg |
| Diastolic blood pressure (DBP) | 60–90 mmHg |
| Mean arterial pressure (MAP) | 70–105 mmHg |
| Pulmonary artery pressure (PAP) (systolic/diastolic) | 15–30/6–12 mmHg |
| Pulmonary artery occlusion pressure (PAOP) (wedge pressure) | 4–12 mmHg |
| Right atrial pressure/central venous pressure (RA/CVP) | 0–8 mmHg |
| Cardiac output (CO) | 4–8 L/min |
| Cardiac index (CI) | 2.5–4.2 L/min/m² |
| Systemic vascular resistance (SVR) | 770–1,500 dyne/sec/cm$^{-5}$ |

If the patient has epicardial pacing wires, atrial wires exit the chest wall on the patient's right and ventricular wires exit the chest wall on the patient's left. These pacing wires should be checked for functioning in case they are needed emergently. If the patient is being paced on arrival to the ICU, pacer settings should be evaluated and documented (Table 9.3).

## ESSENTIAL FACTS

To check to see if epicardial pacer wires are still functioning, connect a temporary pacemaker generator to the lead wires. Set the pacemaker in the DDD mode at a rate higher than the patient's own intrinsic heart rate. Increase milliamps until pacing spikes followed by paced beats are seen on the monitor. This indicates that the epicardial pacing wires are functioning.

### Neurological Assessment

A neuro assessment should be completed, including level of consciousness, pupil size and reaction, and ability to move

## TABLE 9.3 Pacemaker Settings

| First Letter<br>Chamber Paced | Second Letter<br>Chamber Sensed | Third Letter Response<br>After Sensing |
| --- | --- | --- |
| A—atrium | A—atrium | I—pacing inhibited |
| V—ventricle | V—ventricle | T—pacing triggered |
| D—dual (atrium<br>and ventricle) | D—dual (atrium<br>and ventricle) | D—dual (both inhibited and<br>triggered) |
| | O—none | O—none |

extremities. Patients who are intubated or sedated should have as complete a neuro assessment as is possible. Assessing pain is an important part of this assessment. Either patients should self-report their pain, which is the most reliable pain assessment, or a validated behavioral pain scale should be used. Several behavioral pain scales have been validated in critical care patients. These include the Checklist of Nonverbal Pain Indicators (CNPI), the Behavioral Pain Scale (BPS), and the Critical Care Pain Observation Tool (CPOT).

## Respiratory Assessment

Initial assessment should include respiratory rate, symmetry of chest expansion, and breath sounds. Patients who are still intubated should have the placement of the endotracheal tube verified using the marking on the tube. Ventilator settings should also be verified. A baseline chest x-ray should be performed as ordered by the physician to evaluate placement of the endotracheal tube and other devices such as catheters, pacing wires, and chest tubes. A chest x-ray will also show the presence and extent of post-op atelectasis and pneumothorax.

Patients frequently have chest tubes on arrival to the ICU. The type and number of tubes vary based on the surgical procedure performed. One or more chest tubes may be placed in the mediastinal cavity (within the pericardial sac next to the heart) or in the pleural cavity (within the pleural space next to the lungs). Each chest tube should be clearly marked and documented so it is apparent how much drainage is coming from which tube. This is critical when evaluating bleeding. Chest tubes should be attached to –20 cm $H_2O$ wall suction. The type, color, and amount of drainage should be monitored and documented. Patency of these chest tubes must be maintained at all times.

## Fluid and Electrolyte Status

Intake and output from the operating room and during the initial post-op period should be recorded and evaluated to determine the patient's fluid status. Electrolytes should be monitored frequently and kept within a normal range. It is important that the cardiac surgery nurse anticipate third spacing of fluids, which is an increase in edema due to fluid leaving the vascular space and entering the tissues.

**CLINICAL ALERT!** Frequent assessments should be made to ensure dressings, bandages, or sequential compression devices do not become excessively tight during these fluid shifts. These devices can cause severe damage to skin and tissues.

## ESSENTIAL FACTS

The initial physical assessment upon arrival to the ICU is critical to establish a baseline against which to compare future assessments and to uncover potential problems requiring action to prevent complications.

## MAJOR CONCERNS DURING THE INITIAL RECOVERY PERIOD

### Maintaining Hemodynamic Stability

Maintaining an adequate cardiac output is essential to achieving a balance between oxygen supply and demand. Factors affecting cardiac output include preload, afterload, heart rate and rhythm, and contractility.

### Preload

Preload is the amount of volume returning to the right or left side of the heart (ventricular end-diastolic volume). Preload determines the amount of stretch of myocardial fibers just prior to contraction. Owing to the difficulty in directly measuring the volume in the heart, pressure in the ventricle is measured as a way of estimating the volume in the ventricle. Right-sided pre-load may be determined by measuring the CVP. Left-sided pre-load may be found by measuring the PAOP. Decreased left-sided preload is the most common cause of decreased cardiac output in the immediate post-op period. Post-op cardiac surgery patients may have inadequate preload as a result of vasodilation (either due to an inflammatory response caused by cardiopulmonary bypass or due to rewarming), medications, bleeding, third spacing, and urinary output.

## ESSENTIAL FACTS

Third spacing refers to movement of fluid from the vascular space into the tissues, resulting in edema and swelling. Large amounts of fluid may be lost in this manner.

A decrease in preload should be treated with volume reple-tion using crystalloids or colloids. There is no consensus in the literature as to whether one is preferred over the other; usually a combination of crystalloids and colloids is given. The bulk of fluid resuscitation is completed in the first 6 to 8 hours, when the average patient receives 1 to 3 liters of fluid in 250- to 500-mL doses.

Patients may experience surgical or nonsurgical bleeding after cardiac surgery, which may affect preload and decrease cardiac output. Surgical bleeding is caused by poor intraoperative hemostasis and requires return to the operating room to resolve. Nonsurgical bleeding may be caused by inadequate reversal of anticoagulation, platelet dysfunction, or platelet consumption due to medications or cardiopulmonary bypass, and fibrinolysis. Hypertension, hypothermia, and shivering may also contribute to blood loss. Treatment of nonsurgical bleeding includes control of blood pressure and shivering, rewarming, and administration of blood products. (This will be discussed in more detail in Chapter 10.)

If volume repletion and control of bleeding do not increase preload and improve cardiac output, the physician likely will order the addition of a vasopressor. The most commonly used vasopressor is norepinephrine (Levophed). If norepinepherine alone is ineffective, the physician may order vasopressin to increase preload. In post-op cardiac surgery patients experiencing severe vasodilatory shock, methylene blue may be ordered as it is effective in causing vasoconstriction. (See Table 9.4 for additional information on medications.)

**TABLE 9.4 Medications Used to Optimize Cardiac Output**

| Name | Dose | Actions | Side Effects | Nursing Implications |
|---|---|---|---|---|
| Norepinephrine (Levophed) | 0.5–16 mcg/min infusion | Dose-dependent vasoconstriction | Increased myocardial workload and oxygen consumption; hypoperfusion of other organs and peripheral tissues | Usually titrated to a goal mean arterial pressure (MAP) |
| Vasopressin (Pitressin) | 0.01–0.1 units/min infusion | Vasoconstriction | Hypoperfusion of organs; hyponatremia | Given as an adjunct to other vasopressors |
| Methylene blue | 2 mg/kg slow IV push | Vasoconstriction | Hypertension; discolored urine; falsely low pulse oximetry readings (lasting < 10 min) | May be given for severe vasodilatory shock when other vasopressors are ineffective |
| Nitroglycerin (Nitro-Dur; Nitrostat) | Start infusion at 10 mcg/min and titrate in 10 mcg/min increments | Vasodilation (venous > arterial); dilates coronary arteries; improves pulmonary congestion; decreases myocardial oxygen consumption | Rapid-onset hypotension; tachycardia or bradycardia; headache; hypoxemia | Usually titrated to a goal MAP |
| Nitroprusside (Nipride) | 0.3–10 mcg/kg/min infusion | Vasodilation (arterial = venous) | Severe hypotension; coronary steal syndrome; cyanide and thiocyanate toxicity; lactic acidosis | Usually titrated for blood pressure or cardiac index (CI) |
| Hydralazine (Apresoline) | 5–20 mg IV push | Vasodilation (arterial > venous) | Hypotension; tachycardia; with prolonged administration: fever, neuropathies, headaches, lupus-like syndrome (at high doses) | |

*(continued)*

| TABLE 9.4 | Medications Used to Optimize Cardiac Output (continued) | | | |
|---|---|---|---|---|
| Name | Dose | Actions | Side Effects | Nursing Implications |
| Amiodarone (Cordarone) | Loading: 150 mg IV over 10 minutes followed by 1 mg/min for 6 hours, then 0.5 mg/min infusion | Antiarrhythmic | Bradycardia; hypotension; with chronic administration: thyroid dysfunction, pulmonary fibrosis, skin discoloration, hepatitis | Multiple drug interactions |
| Dobutamine (Dobutrex) | 2–20 mcg/kg/min infusion | Inotrope and vasodilator | Hypotension; tachycardia; ventricular dysrhythmias; myocardial ischemia | |
| Milrinone (Primacor) | Loading: 50 mcg/kg Infusion: 0.125–0.5 mcg/kg/min | Inotrope and vasodilator | Hypotension; tachycardia | Loading dose may be omitted to avoid profound hypotension |
| Dopamine (Intropin) | 1–2 mcg/kg/min | Dilation of renal, mesenteric, cerebral, and coronary arteries | As dose increases: tachycardia; increased myocardial oxygen demand; decreased renal perfusion; ventricular arrhythmias | Dose-dependent effect |
| | 5–10 mcg/kg/min | Inotrope | | Maximum infusion 40 mcg/kg/min |
| | 10–20 mcg/kg/min | Vasoconstriction | | |
| Epinephrine (Adrenaline) | 1–10 mcg/min | Inotrope; positive chronotrope | Tachycardia; arrhythmias; metabolic acidosis; severe hyperglycemia | Vasodilation seen at lower doses; vasoconstriction seen at higher doses |
| Isoproterenol (Isoprenaline) | 1–4 mcg/min | Inotrope; positive chronotrope | Tachycardia; lethal ventricular dysrhythmias; hypotension | Do not use if myocardial ischemia present |

▶ **NURSING IMPLICATIONS:** Measuring hemodynamic parameters and assessing the patient to determine if the patient has adequate preload are important functions of the cardiac surgery nurse. Notifying the physician of decreased preload and titrating medications within ordered parameters are critical to maintaining adequate cardiac output.

## ESSENTIAL FACTS

> Decreased preload is the most common cause of low cardiac output in post-op cardiac surgery patients. Maintaining an optimal CVP and PAOP by fluid resuscitation should be the first action taken when attempting to improve cardiac output.

### Afterload

Afterload is the amount of force that must be overcome to eject blood from the ventricles. Increased afterload may cause metabolic acidosis due to tissue hypoperfusion and decreased cardiac output. An increase in afterload may be caused by hypertension, medications that cause vasoconstriction, hypothermia, pain, and increased SVR. Immediately after operation, cardiac surgery patients are particularly prone to hypertension due to hypothermia and catecholamine release, which cause vasoconstriction. Afterload may be reduced by administration of a vasodilator, rewarming strategies, or by use of a device such as an intraaortic balloon pump.

Several medications are used to reduce afterload and thus increase cardiac output. Nitroglycerin is a vasodilator that has a more potent effect on veins than on arteries. Nitroglycerin also dilates coronary arteries, prevents vasospasm, and decreases pulmonary congestion and myocardial oxygen consumption. Nitroprusside (Nipride) is a potent vasodilator that dilates both veins and arteries. It is most beneficial to patients who have elevated left ventricular filling pressures and a marginal cardiac output. Hydralazine preferentially dilates arteries and is a potent afterload reducer. (See Table 9.4 for additional information on medications.)

▶ **NURSING IMPLICATIONS:** Measuring hemodynamic parameters as ordered by the physician and searching for other causes of increased afterload are important nursing functions. The physician should be notified of increased afterload so appropriate medications and treatments to reduce afterload may be ordered.

### ESSENTIAL FACTS

When attempting to improve cardiac output, afterload should be considered once preload is optimized. The cause of increased afterload should be considered when choosing an intervention.

## Dysrhythmias

Dysrhythmias in post-op cardiac surgery patients are commonly caused by ischemia, electrolyte imbalances, decreased perfusion, hypoxemia, and medications. Dysrhythmias frequently cause hemodynamic instability, and heart rate and rhythm should be monitored closely. In post-op cardiac surgery patients, atrial arrhythmias are the most common, but ventricular arrhythmias and heart blocks are also commonly seen. Epicardial temporary pacing wires are frequently placed during surgery in the event they are needed to treat dysrhythmias. If dysrhythmias occur, normal sinus rhythm or a paced rhythm should be restored as soon as possible. For lethal arrhythmias, advanced cardiac life support (ACLS) algorithms should be followed.

Antiarrhythmic medications are frequently given to restore a normal rhythm. Amiodarone (Cordarone) is frequently used in post-op cardiac surgery patients because of its ability to quickly convert both atrial and ventricular arrhythmias to a normal sinus rhythm. To accomplish this, a loading dose must be given followed by daily administration. (See Table 9.4 for additional information.) For dysrhythmias causing hemodynamic instability, cardioversion in conjunction with amiodarone is often used. Electrolyte replacement is also critical to prevent dysrhythmias. Serum potassium level should be kept between 4 and 5 mEq/L and serum magnesium level should be kept above 2 mEq/L.

▶ **NURSING IMPLICATIONS:** The cardiac surgery nurse plays a critical role in recognizing dysrhythmias and responding quickly, either by following orders already in place or by notifying the physician so treatment can begin in a timely manner. Nurses should monitor electrolytes and either follow existing replacement orders or call the physician to obtain orders to replace potassium and magnesium.

## ESSENTIAL FACTS

> To maintain an acceptable cardiac output, dysrhythmias should be treated quickly and heart rate and rhythm should be restored.

### Contractility

Contractility refers to the strength and speed of heart muscle contraction and is critical to a patient's cardiac output. Contractility may be affected by myocardial stunning, preload, afterload, and heart rate and rhythm. When cardiac output is inadequate despite efforts to optimize preload and afterload and to normalize heart rate and rhythm, positive inotropes may be given to increase contractility and improve output.

Dobutamine (Dobutrex) is a first-line inotropic medication used in cardiac surgery patients. It improves contractility and also causes vasodilation, which decreases afterload and improves coronary artery blood flow. The vasodilatory effect may also cause hypotension, and a vasopressor may be needed to support blood pressure. Milrinone (Primacor) is a phosphodiesterase inhibitor, which increases contractility and causes vasodilation. It frequently causes hypotension, especially with an initial bolus, and patients may require vasopressor support to maintain blood pressure. Dopamine (Intropin) has different effects at different dose ranges. A positive inotropic effect and subsequent increase in cardiac output is seen with an infusion rate of 5 to 10 mcg/kg/min. The dose of dopamine should be no more than is needed for the desired effect. Epinephrine (adrenaline) is used to improve contractility and increase heart rate in post-op patients with cardiogenic shock. Epinephrine causes vasodilation at low doses and vasoconstriction at higher doses. Isoproterenol (isoprenaline) is another medication that improves contractility and increases heart rate. It also causes vasodilation, so should not be used in hypotensive patients. Isoproterenol is most often used in post-op cardiac surgery patients to treat bradycardias. (See Table 9.4 for additional information on medications.)

Intracellular calcium is important to the contractile ability of the heart. For this reason, calcium chloride is often given to patients in the operating room to wean them off cardiopulmonary bypass. Blood products contain citrate (used to prevent coagulation of the blood), which binds to ionized calcium in the patient's blood when administered.

**CLINICAL ALERT!** Patients who receive blood products may develop citrate toxicity, low levels of ionized calcium, and subsequent myocardial depression and decreased cardiac output. When needed, calcium chloride should be administered cautiously, as per physician orders, 100 to 200 mg at a time, owing to its potential to cause lethal dysrhythmias.

▶ **NURSING IMPLICATIONS:** If preload and afterload are optimized and cardiac output remains low, the cardiac surgery nurse should notify the physician so medications that improve contractility may be ordered.

## ESSENTIAL FACTS

Once other measures have been taken and cardiac output remains inadequate, positive inotropes may be administered to increase myocardial contractility and improve cardiac output.

## Hypothermia

Patients are considered hypothermic if their core temperature is less than 96.8°F (36°C). Patients may be intentionally cooled in the operating room to decrease ischemia during cardiopulmonary bypass and cardiac standstill. However, post-op hypothermia may cause several potential problems. Post-op patients with a core temperature less than 96.8°F (36°C) may require prolonged ventilation and have increased SVR (afterload), dysrhythmias, hypertension, tachycardia, decreased preload, impaired contractility, and graft spasm. Hypothermia disrupts the clotting cascade, leading to more transfusions of blood products. Drug metabolism may be altered and patients may take longer to emerge from anesthesia. Hypothermia may also cause delayed wound healing.

Shivering is a detrimental consequence of hypothermia because it causes dramatically increased oxygen demands and buildup of carbon dioxide ($CO_2$). The use of paralytic and anesthetic agents may make it difficult to recognize shivering.

**CLINICAL ALERT!** Oxygen saturation, end-tidal $CO_2$, hemodynamics, blood loss, and perfusion should be monitored closely for indications of increased oxygen consumption and $CO_2$ production, which may signal shivering.

Since hypothermia and shivering are detrimental, it is important to attain normothermia as soon as possible and avoid or treat shivering. Warming blankets, warm ambient room temperature, and warm oxygen and fluids have been used effectively to rewarm hypothermic post-op patients. Meperidine (Demerol) is commonly used to treat shivering.

▶ **NURSING IMPLICATIONS:** The cardiac surgery nurse plays an important role in recognizing hypothermia immediately after surgery and instituting rewarming strategies. The nurse is also in the unique position to recognize shivering early and to institute treatment strategies.

## *ESSENTIAL FACTS*

Hypothermia and shivering are detrimental to post-op cardiac surgery patients. Normothermia should be reached as soon as possible and shivering should be aggressively treated.

### Respiratory Management

Respiratory management is critical for post-op cardiac surgery patients. Some patients, especially those with off-pump surgeries, may be extubated in the operating room. However, most patients arrive in the ICU intubated and on a ventilator. The goal for these patients is early extubation. Weaning and extubation protocols vary, but the goal for all post-op cardiac surgery patients should be to extubate within 4 to 12 hours after surgery.

Extubation criteria often include heart rate less than 140, respiratory rate less than 25, normothermia, and absence of ischemia. Patients should be alert and cooperative, with a cough and gag reflex. They should be able to breathe spontaneously while maintaining adequate oxygen saturation and arterial blood gas readings. Patients should be able to demonstrate adequate muscle strength by maintaining a head lift for at least 5 seconds. Opioids should be used cautiously prior to extubation, as they may reduce respiratory effort and decrease rate and depth of respirations. However, it is also important to ensure adequate pain control.

When the patient is ready for extubation, the mouth should be suctioned and the device securing the tube should be removed. The endotracheal tube cuff should be deflated with a syringe and an air leak verified. The patient should be told to take a deep breath and cough. The tube should be removed toward the end of the cough. Supplemental humidified oxygen should be administered—typically low-flow oxygen via nasal cannula.

Patients who received an inhaled anesthetic during surgery and who are extubated in the operating room require a stir-up regimen immediately post-op. These agents cause respiratory depression and are blown off through ventilation of the lungs with oxygen. Stir-up is accomplished by administering oxygen, elevating the head of the bed, and asking the patient to breathe deeply and cough at regular intervals. This facilitates the removal of the inhalation agent from the body.

▶ **NURSING IMPLICATIONS:** Although in many institutions a respiratory therapist monitors the ventilator or performs extubation, the cardiac surgery nurse coordinates and facilitates the process. The nurse needs to understand ventilator settings and work with the physician and respiratory therapist to ensure that settings are right for each patient. The nurse also needs to assess the patient for readiness to extubate and move the process along, if necessary.

*ESSENTIAL FACTS*

Extubation within 4 to 12 hours after cardiac surgery reduces respiratory complications and should be a goal for all patients.

## Complications Related to Extubation

Complications after extubation may include laryngospasm, noncardiogenic pulmonary edema, bronchospasm, hypoventilation, and hypoxia. Fortunately, these complications are uncommon.

Laryngospasm is a spasm or sudden narrowing of the vocal cords. This causes a partial airway obstruction that leads to wheezing, stridor, tachypnea, dyspnea, and use of accessory muscles. Patients should be encouraged to cough, as this may alleviate a partial obstruction. Laryngospasm may also lead to noncardiogenic pulmonary edema. When a patient forcefully attempts an inspiration against an airway obstruction, it causes an increase in intrathoracic pressure and may lead to protein and fluid accumulation in the alveolar sacs. This type of pulmonary edema typically has a rapid onset and may be manifest by agitation, tachypnea, tachycardia, decreased oxygen saturation, audible crackles, and pink, frothy sputum. The patient may need reintubation until these problems are resolved.

**CLINICAL ALERT!** Patients with pulmonary edema may require administration of diuretics as ordered by the physician.

Bronchospasm refers to constriction of the bronchial smooth muscle and may occur after extubation. Symptoms include wheezing, dyspnea, and tachypnea. Bronchospasm is usually resolved with a bronchodilator and humidified oxygen, but in severe cases may require a physician's order for administration of a muscle relaxant, epinephrine, lidocaine, or hydrocortisone to relax the airway.

Hypoventilation is common in the post-op period and may be caused by medications or the surgical procedure. Hypoventilation may lead to hypoxia and decreased oxygen saturation. Other signs and symptoms of hypoxia include cyanosis, agitation or somnolence, tachycardia or bradycardia, and hypertension or hypotension. Hypoxia can have serious consequences, including dysrhythmias, myocardial ischemia and dysfunction of other organ systems. Reintubation and ventilation may be required until the causes of hypoventilation can be reversed.

▶ **NURSING IMPLICATIONS:** The nurse should be at the bedside after extubation to observe for any complications. The cardiac surgery nurse should be knowledgeable about potential complications and prepared to intervene immediately if necessary.

## ESSENTIAL FACTS

Complications after extubation are uncommon but potentially life-threatening. Patients must be monitored closely for indications of obstructed airway or inadequate ventilation after extubation.

## COMPLICATIONS RELATED TO ANESTHESIA

### Post-Op Nausea and Vomiting

Nausea and vomiting are common immediately after surgery due to medications given during surgery. Post-op nausea and vomiting (PONV) may lead to aspiration, bleeding, electrolyte abnormalities, and dehydration. Medications that may be used to decrease the occurrence of PONV include ondansetron (Zofran), promethazine (Phenergan), and prochlorperazine (Compazine). If several doses of these medications administered per physician's order do not relieve PONV, the anesthesiologist should be notified.

## Malignant Hyperthermia

Malignant hyperthermia (MH) is a life-threatening, genetic condition caused by certain anesthetics, depolarizing skeletal muscle relaxants, and stress. The most common triggering agents are halothane, enflurane, isoflurane, desflurane, and succinylcholine. When triggered, this genetic condition causes prolonged skeletal muscle contraction, leading to a hypermetabolic state and hyperthermia. MH usually begins during the induction of anesthesia and manifests in the operating room, but it may occur anytime within the first 24 hours post-op.

**CLINICAL ALERT!** Prompt recognition and treatment are critical in effectively managing this condition. Signs and symptoms include muscle rigidity of the jaw, tachypnea, tachycardia, elevated $CO_2$, cyanosis, respiratory and metabolic acidosis, elevated creatinine phosphokinase, and hyperkalemia. Temperature elevation, bleeding, and rhabdomyolysis are late signs.

Treatment of MH includes removal of triggering agents and immediate administration of intravenous dantrolene sodium (Dantrium). A typical physician order includes administration of a loading dose followed by a dose every 4 hours for at least 48 hours. Additional interventions, which must be ordered by a physician, include hyperventilation, cooling blankets, administration of oxygen and sodium bicarbonate, and maintenance of fluid and electrolyte balance.

▶ **NURSING IMPLICATIONS:** Since MH is a life-threatening condition that can occur quickly, the cardiac surgery nurse needs to be aware of this complication and be prepared to act quickly. If unsure if the patient is experiencing MH, the nurse may seek assistance from operating room nurses or the anesthesiologist, who may have more experience with the condition.

## ESSENTIAL FACTS

> MH is a rare but life-threatening condition that occurs after administration of certain anesthetic agents. Prompt recognition and treatment are critical.

## Pseudocholinesterase Deficiency

A small percentage of patients lack the enzyme pseudocholinesterase, which is responsible for metabolizing medications such as succinylcholine. Patients with this enzyme deficiency who receive these anesthetic agents experience a prolonged reaction to the agents. They may have sustained muscle paralysis and remain apneic for as long as 48 hours. Management includes mechanical ventilation and emotional support until the effects of the anesthetic wear off.

## ESSENTIAL FACTS

> The initial post-op recovery period is critical for cardiac surgery patients. Careful assessment and expert nursing care are important for minimizing complications. Optimizing cardiac output and anticipating and preventing complications are the primary goals of the immediate post-op recovery period.

## BIBLIOGRAPHY

Hardin, S. R., & Kaplow, R. (Eds.). (2010). *Cardiac surgery essentials for critical care nursing.* Sudbury, MA: Jones & Bartlett.

Katz, E. A. (2007). Pharmacologic management of the postoperative cardiac surgery patient. *Critical Care Nursing Clinics of North America, 19,* 487–496.

Opie, L. H., & Gersh, B. J. (Eds.). (2005). *Drugs for the heart* (6th ed.). Philadelphia, PA: Elsevier Saunders.

# 10

## Complications: Initial Postoperative Period

*Advances in surgical techniques and anesthetic agents allow many patients to recover quickly and move from the intensive care unit (ICU) in shorter periods of time. However, many patients still experience complications of surgery and require intensive nursing care in the initial post-op period. Patients presenting for surgery are increasingly older with more risk factors and underlying comorbid conditions, which increases the risk of complications after surgery. Patients who experience complications often have a longer ICU and hospital stay and may have a higher risk of death than patients who do not experience surgical complications. Nurses must be extra vigilant to observe for and treat potential complications as early as possible.*

## Objectives

In this chapter, you will learn:

1. Prevention and treatment of common post-op cardiac surgery complications
2. Assessment, laboratory, and x-ray findings that may signal potential complications

# CARDIAC COMPLICATIONS

Cardiac output (CO) is determined by several factors. Decreased preload and decreased contractility (myocardial depression) are the two most common causes of low CO after cardiac surgery. Bleeding, increased urinary output, increased capillary permeability (causing fluid to be lost into the tissues), decreased ventricular compliance (lower ventricular filling volumes), or cardiac tamponade may cause a decrease in preload. Decreased contractility may be caused by myocardial depression, myocardial stunning, acidosis, hypoxemia, or by the inflammatory response produced because of surgery.

## Low Cardiac Output

The most common cause of mortality after surgery is a low CO state (Jacobson, Marzlin, & Webner, 2007). It be difficult to manage low CO after surgery, as there are so many potential causes. Recognizing the factors that lead to a decrease in CO and taking action to improve CO after surgery are critical nursing functions during this initial period.

### Prevention

Once the patient is in the ICU, prevention may not be possible. It is critical that a decrease in CO be recognized early and treated promptly.

### Assessment

Signs and symptoms of impaired CO include altered mental status, hypotension, decreased mean arterial pressure (MAP), tachycardia, decreased pulses, lengthened capillary refill time, narrow pulse pressure, cool extremities, and oliguria or anuria.

### Diagnostics

If available, a pulmonary artery catheter or continuous CO device may be used to estimate CO. If CO is not adequate, a mixed venous oxygen saturation ($SvO_2$) will be lower than normal (less than 70%). $SvO_2$ is the percentage of hemoglobin saturated with oxygen found in blood returning to the heart (right atrium or pulmonary artery).

A low reading indicates hypoperfusion or an increased metabolic rate. If CO is not adequate, metabolic acidosis and an increase in serum lactic acid will also be found.

## Intervention

Inadequate CO may be caused by inadequate preload, elevated afterload, alterations in heart rate or rhythm, myocardial depression (poor contractility), or a combination of these factors. The first factor to be addressed when CO is low is preload. Fluid resuscitation with crystalloids and colloids should be continued until there is evidence of adequate intravascular volume. This would be demonstrated by a central venous pressure (CVP) or right atrial pressure of 8 mmHg and a pulmonary artery occlusion pressure (PAOP) of 15 mmHg. If preload is adequate and CO remains poor, afterload should be examined and optimized. A number of intravenous medications may be administered as per physician order to decrease afterload and improve CO. Heart rate and rhythm are critical for maintaining CO. If the patient experiences a dysrhythmia, bradyarrhythmia, or tachyarrhythmia, heart rate and rhythm should be returned to normal. If all other parameters have been optimized and CO remains inadequate, an inotropic medication may be ordered by a physician to improve CO. (See Chapter 9 for a more detailed description of optimizing hemodynamics, including medications used to improve CO.)

▶ **NURSING IMPLICATIONS:** The cardiac surgery nurse plays an important role in recognizing low CO states and intervening based on physician orders. After surgery, patients typically have orders for various vasoactive, inotropic, and antiarrhythmic medications. These need to be administered according to the surgeon's orders and the hospital and unit policy to maintain CO. Cardiac surgery nurses must have an intimate knowledge of how these medications work and when to administer or titrate each one. The new cardiac surgery nurse should work with experienced nurses until these skills are learned. (See Chapter 9 for tips on administering various medications to maintain CO.)

## *ESSENTIAL FACTS*

Decreased CO is a major problem in the immediate post-op period. Maintaining adequate CO is one of the primary nursing goals during this period and reduces other complications and organ failure.

# Myocardial Ischemia and Infarction

Myocardial ischemia and infarction may occur after cardiac surgery for a number of reasons. Risk factors include older age, multiple comorbidities, large extent of coronary artery disease, decreased left ventricular function, redo surgery, long cardiopulmonary bypass time, and bypass surgery combined with another cardiac surgical procedure, such as valve surgery.

Myocardial ischemia may occur due to incomplete revascularization, poor myocardial protection during surgery, coronary vasospasm, or embolism. Myocardial infarction (MI) may be due to thrombosis (clot formation in a coronary artery or graft) or acute closure of a bypass graft. The incidence of MI after coronary artery bypass surgery is between 1% and 5% (Coventry, 2014).

## Prevention

Patients should be started on aspirin (or clopidogrel if aspirin is not tolerated) prior to or within 6 hours after surgery for prevention of saphenous vein graft closure and thrombosis leading to MI (Hillis et al., 2011).

## Assessment

Frequently, there are no abnormal assessment findings. Diagnosis is made based on 12-lead electrocardiogram (ECG) and laboratory findings. In the setting of vasospasm, there may be a sudden decrease in CO. (See the section on vasospasm for more information.)

## Diagnostics

A 12-lead ECG frequently reveals ST-segment elevation in a specific coronary artery distribution, new Q waves, new bundle branch block, complete heart block, or ventricular dysrhythmias. If ST-segment elevation is seen in every lead, this may be caused by pericarditis, which is common after cardiac surgery and does not indicate an MI.

Cardiac markers are elevated in the presence of MI. However, elevations in cardiac markers due to surgical injury to the heart must be taken into account. As a general rule, a creatine kinase–myocardial band (CK-MB) level that is 10 times the upper limit of normal or a troponin level greater than 15 to 20 mcg/dL indicates an MI.

Patients who experience post-op myocardial ischemia or MI often follow the same post-op course as other patients. Physician orders may include administration of nitroglycerin and beta-blockers if blood pressure will support the administration of these medications. Inotropes should be used sparingly if at all, as they increase myocardial oxygen demand. If an intervention is needed to improve CO, an intraaortic balloon pump may be used to assist the pumping ability of the heart and improve coronary artery blood flow.

If acute graft closure is suspected as the cause of MI, emergency coronary angiography with percutaneous coronary intervention may be indicated. (See Chapter 1 for a description of percutaneous coronary intervention.) Surgical reexploration may also be required.

▶ **NURSING IMPLICATIONS:** Coronary vasospasm and myocardial injury or infarction may initially present in the same way. Administration of nitroglycerin, as ordered by the physician, is appropriate treatment for both. It can be difficult to tell if the patient is experiencing vasospasm or ischemia from another cause. However, with the administration of a vasodilator, coronary vasospasm should be relieved quickly and cardiac enzymes should not be elevated above what is normal after cardiac surgery. (See the next section for more information on vasospasm.)

*ESSENTIAL FACTS*

The goal when treating myocardial ischemia or infarction after cardiac surgery is to minimize damage to the myocardium and maintain adequate CO.

## Coronary Vasospasm

Vasospasm is a potential cause of sudden cardiovascular collapse in the early post-op period and is often unrecognized. Spasm may occur in saphenous vein grafts, internal mammary or radial artery grafts, or in native coronary arteries. The cause of spasm in these vessels is unclear. Vasospasm is more likely to occur in radial artery grafts.

## Prevention

Steps are taken in the operating room to prevent spasm. As grafts are prepared for implantation, manipulation is kept to a minimum. Prior to implantation, radial artery grafts are typically soaked in a solution designed to prevent vasospasm. Patients are often sent out of the operating room on infusions of medications that help to prevent spasm, such as nitroglycerin (Tridil) or diltiazem (Cardizem), especially when radial artery grafts are used.

## Assessment

**CLINICAL ALERT!** Vasospasm of coronary arteries or grafts typically presents as sudden hypotension with decreased CO.

## Diagnostics

A 12-lead ECG demonstrates ST-segment elevation in multiple leads.

## Intervention

Coronary vasospasm often resolves without intervention. If these patients become hemodynamically unstable, supportive care should be instituted. Administration of vasodilators such as calcium channel blockers or nitroglycerin, as per physician's orders, may help to resolve vasospasm.

▶ **NURSING IMPLICATIONS:** Patients with radial artery grafts should be on a medication to prevent graft spasm. If a patient decompensates suddenly, a 12-lead ECG should be performed to evaluate for ischemia.

## ESSENTIAL FACTS

Coronary vasospasm may cause sudden hypotension and cardiovascular collapse. It may resolve spontaneously or require administration of nitroglycerin or calcium channel blockers.

The pericardial sac is entered during surgery and is usually not sewn back up. This creates a communication between the pericardial space and the mediastinum. If blood accumulates in the mediastinum, this may lead to cardiac tamponade. Cardiac tamponade is an accumulation of blood to the point where pressure is placed on the heart (Figure 10.1). This pressure constricts the thin-walled atria and reduces the amount of blood that fills the ventricles (reduces preload). This may cause a sudden and profound drop in CO.

Several things may lead to cardiac tamponade in the early post-op period. The most common is clotting of mediastinal chest tubes, which causes blood to accumulate and leads to the development of cardiac tamponade. Also, an anastamosis (point where graft is sewn into a coronary artery) may not be fully sealed or may fail suddenly, causing a rapid accumulation of blood in the mediastinum. Early cardiac tamponade typically occurs during the first 12 hours post-op.

### Prevention

Maintaining patency of mediastinal chest tubes is important to prevent cardiac tamponade.

### Assessment

Cardiac tamponade may be difficult to recognize in the early post-op period. Hypotension, tachycardia, and elevated filling pressures

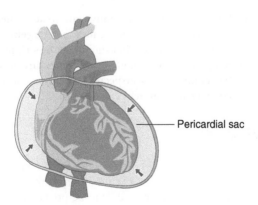

Pericardial sac

**FIGURE 10.1** Cardiac tamponade.

are seen, but are common in most cardiac surgery patients during this period. A high index of suspicion for cardiac tamponade assists in early recognition.

**CLINICAL ALERT!** Key clinical signs and symptoms include a sudden drop in output from mediastinal chest tubes, dyspnea, hypotension, tachycardia, low CO, narrowing pulse pressure, increased CVP, altered mental status, diaphoresis, anxiety, and restlessness.

## Diagnostics

Chest x-ray may reveal cardiac or mediastinal enlargement. A 12-lead ECG may indicate low voltage or electrical alternans. If cardiac tamponade is suspected, a bedside echocardiogram should be obtained as soon as possible, as this is the best way to diagnose cardiac tamponade.

## Intervention

Cardiac tamponade in the immediate post-op period necessitates immediate surgical reexploration to determine the source of bleeding and evacuate accumulated blood. If cardiac arrest is imminent, emergency resternotomy may be performed. This typically involves the surgeon and operating room personnel opening the chest at the bedside. The ICU nurse should be prepared to assist with setting up a sterile field and gathering a specialized instrument tray for the surgical team.

▶ **NURSING IMPLICATIONS:** It is important to keep chest tubes draining after cardiac surgery. Chest tubes may be gently milked if needed to keep them draining, but should not be stripped. Stripping chest tubes produces very high negative pressure in the chest cavity. If cardiac tamponade is suspected, the physician should be notified immediately so treatment can begin.

## ESSENTIAL FACTS

Cardiac tamponade is a life-threatening early complication after cardiac surgery. Nurses should watch for the signs that may indicate cardiac tamponade and be prepared to intervene early when it is suspected.

Bleeding after cardiac surgery is a common post-op complication. Patients may experience surgical or nonsurgical bleeding after cardiac surgery. Surgical bleeding is caused by poor intraoperative hemostasis whereas nonsurgical bleeding may be caused by inadequate reversal of anticoagulation, platelet dysfunction or platelet consumption due to medications or cardiopulmonary bypass, and fibrinolysis. Hypertension after surgery may place strain on suture lines and sites of anastomosis. In extreme cases, grafts may become dislodged from where they have been sutured. Hypothermia and shivering may also contribute to blood loss.

Transfusion of blood products after cardiac surgery is common. However, numerous large observational studies have indicated that administration of red blood cells during or after cardiac surgery is an independent risk factor for surgical complications, including decreased CO and death (Hillis et al., 2011).

**CLINICAL ALERT!** Transfusion of red blood cells has been associated with higher infection rates, including sternal infections, transmission of viruses, transfusion-related acute lung injury (TRALI), renal failure, volume overload, and increased mortality.

## Prevention

Aggressive attempts should be made to limit bleeding and hemodilutional anemia to reduce the need for transfusion of red blood cells. Physician's orders include withholding antiplatelet and antithrombotic medications prior to surgery (with the exception of aspirin). Patients should be rewarmed after surgery, blood pressure should be controlled, and agitation should be minimized. When bleeding is suspected or observed, the source of bleeding should be investigated and treated. Aggressive treatment with platelets and fresh frozen plasma based on the results of coagulation lab results can replace clotting factors lost due to bleeding and reduce the need for red blood cell transfusion. To minimize the use of blood products, especially red blood cells, many institutions have blood conservation protocols with guidelines for when to transfuse.

## Assessment

Severe post-op bleeding affects preload, contributing to hypotension and decreased CO. Chest tube drainage amounts need to be monitored closely for excessive bleeding. Chest tube drainage should be recorded every 15 minutes for the first 2 hours after surgery and every hour thereafter. The patient may need surgical exploration for bleeding if chest tubes drainage exceeds 200 mL/hr over 4 hours, 300 mL/hr over 2 to 3 hours, 400 mL/hr over 1 hour, or more than 1,000 mL in the first 3 to 4 hours. The acute onset of bleeding (more than 300 mL/hr) after a stable period of minimal bleeding requires surgical exploration (Jacobson et al., 2007). Return to the operating room for bleeding occurs in 1% to 5% of cardiac surgery cases (Coventry, 2014).

## Diagnostics

A complete blood count should be performed immediately after surgery. Often, hemoglobin, hematocrit, and platelet levels are low, owing to hemodilution, blood loss during surgery, and consumption of platelets during cardiopulmonary bypass. If persistent bleeding is suspected, physician orders will include drawing blood for hemoglobin and hematocrit levels and comparing the results to those drawn immediately after surgery. If these levels are falling, it is an indication of bleeding. Coagulation factors, including prothrombin time/international normalized ratio (PT/INR) and activated partial thromboplastin time (aPTT), should be drawn to help determine the cause of bleeding.

## Intervention

Surgical bleeding requires return to the operating room for resolution. Treatment of nonsurgical bleeding includes control of blood pressure and shivering, rewarming, and administration of blood products and coagulation factors as per physician orders. Increasing the amount of positive end-expiratory pressure (PEEP) on the ventilator may increase pressure in the mediastinum and limit microvascular mediastinal bleeding. If increasing PEEP is effective, results will be seen within an hour (Jacobson et al., 2007).

Packed red blood cells and platelets should be given based on institutional blood conservation guidelines. Administration of fresh frozen plasma may be ordered to provide a supply of coagulation factors and may help reduce bleeding and the need for additional packed red blood cells. If the effects of heparin given in the operating room have not been adequately reversed (aPTT is elevated), protamine sulfate may be given. Administration of desmopressin (DDAVP) may be ordered to improve platelet function, and aminocaproic acid (Amicar) may help with post-op coagulopathies by reversing fibrinolysis. If bleeding cannot be stopped by using these therapies, administration of recombinant factor VIIa (Novoseven) may be considered to obtain hemostasis.

▶ **NURSING IMPLICATIONS:** Nurses should take all possible steps to prevent bleeding. Orders to give antiplatelet or antithrombotic medications prior to surgery should be questioned, especially if clopidogrel (Plavix), prasugrel (Effient), ticagrelor (Brilinta), or warfarin (Coumadin) have been ordered. Patients should be rewarmed immediately after surgery if they are not warm on arrival to the ICU. Blood pressure should be maintained within the range ordered by the physician.

The cardiac surgery nurse should maintain a high index of suspicion for bleeding. It is critical to recognize bleeding early and search for a source. If bleeding from chest tubes is excessive or if a source of bleeding cannot be recognized and treated with existing orders, the surgeon should be notified.

## ESSENTIAL FACTS

Bleeding after cardiac surgery is common and may affect blood pressure and CO. The cause of bleeding should be investigated and treated as quickly as possible, avoiding transfusion of red blood cells whenever possible.

## PULMONARY COMPLICATIONS

There are multiple factors that place cardiac surgery patients at risk for pulmonary complications.

**CLINICAL ALERT!** Preexisting conditions that put patients at higher risk include smoking, age greater than 65 years, obesity, diabetes, preexisting lung disease (e.g., chronic obstructive pulmonary disease [COPD]), heart failure, and left ventricular dysfunction. Procedure-related factors include general anesthesia, intubation and ventilation, lung deflation and manipulation during surgery, use of the internal mammary artery, cooling, use of cardiopulmonary bypass, and a midline sternotomy incision. Inadequate pain control after surgery may also play a role.

# Atelectasis

Atelectasis is a collapse of the alveolar sacs in the lower parts of the lungs that commonly occurs after surgery. This is especially common in post-op cardiac surgery patients who have had one or both lungs intentionally collapsed during surgery and occurs most commonly in the left lower lobe. Atelectasis is associated with decreased lung compliance, impaired oxygen exchange, and some degree of lung injury.

## Prevention

Atelectasis develops in the operating room and is usually present on admission to the ICU. The post-op focus is on identification and treatment.

## Assessment

Lung sounds are diminished in the bases, especially on the left side.

## Diagnostics

Pulse oximetry readings are usually not affected, but may be decreased if atelectasis is severe. A chest x-ray may show signs of atelectasis.

## Intervention

The goal is to reexpand collapsed alveoli. Deep breathing and coughing should be encouraged frequently. Adequate pain control is important for encouraging patients to breathe deeply. As soon as the patient is able, incentive spirometry should be done every hour while awake. The inspiratory volume (number the patient is able to reach on the incentive spirometer) should be documented so that improvement can be verified.

Increasing patient activity is important for resolving post-op atelectasis. As soon as possible, patients should be sitting in a chair, since this assists with lung expansion. Early ambulation is important for lung expansion and recovery from cardiac surgery. Even if transfer out of the ICU is delayed, patients should be assisted to ambulate when able.

▶ **NURSING IMPLICATIONS:** The cardiac surgery nurse plays a critical role in educating and encouraging patients to perform the exercises necessary for lung expansion. Careful assessment of pain and judicious administration of ordered pain medications remove a major barrier to coughing, deep breathing, and ambulating.

*ESSENTIAL FACTS*

Almost all patients have some degree of atelectasis after cardiac surgery. Having patients cough, take deep breaths, and ambulate reexpands lung tissue and helps to resolve atelectasis

## Pleural Effusion

A pleural effusion is a collection of fluid in the pleural space (Figure 10.2). Pleural effusions are common in post-op cardiac surgery patients. They are usually noted in the left lower lobe but may also be seen bilaterally. A pleural effusion usually results

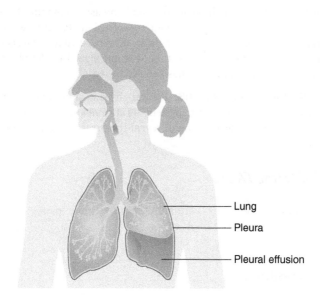

Lung

Pleura

Pleural effusion

**FIGURE 10.2** Pleural effusion.

from the intentional collapse of one or both lungs during surgery and increased capillary permeability due to cardiopulmonary bypass. This complication usually develops within the first 24 hours.

## Prevention

Since pleural effusions are a consequence of surgical interventions in the operating room, the post-op focus is on identification and treatment.

## Assessment

Lung sounds are diminished. If the pleural effusion is large or if the patient has preexisting lung disease, patients may experience dyspnea, especially with exertion.

## Diagnostics

Pulse oximetry may be affected if the pleural effusion is large. Pleural effusions will be visible on chest x-ray.

## Intervention

Most post-op pleural effusions are small and asymptomatic. These usually resolve over time without intervention. Patients with a large or symptomatic pleural effusion may need thoracentesis or chest tube insertion if a chest tube was not placed in the pleural space during surgery or if it has been removed.

▶ **NURSING IMPLICATIONS:** Pleural effusion should be considered for patients who are experiencing dyspnea, either at rest or with exertion. A chest x-ray will reveal the presence and extent of a pleural effusion.

## ESSENTIAL FACTS

Pleural effusions after cardiac surgery are common and usually resolve without intervention.

## Pneumothorax

A pneumothorax is air in the pleural space. A pneumothorax may occur after cardiac surgery due to an injury that occurred during surgery, barotrauma to one or both lungs during mechanical ventilation, or the puncture of a lung during central line insertion. Pneumothorax following cardiac surgery is relatively rare, but when it does occur it usually manifests in the immediate post-op period. Typically, the left lung is involved after dissection of a left internal mammary artery for use as a bypass graft, but a pneumothorax may develop on the right side if the pleura on the right side is cut, either accidentally or when the right internal mammary artery is dissected.

If air pressure builds up in the plural space, a tension pneumothorax may develop (Figure 10.3). This may occur rapidly if a patient with a pneumothorax is placed on mechanical ventilation.

### Prevention

Keeping PEEP low during mechanical ventilation, when possible, helps prevent some instances of pneumothorax.

### Assessment

Breath sounds may be diminished in the presence of a pneumothorax. If a patient develops a tension pneumothorax, the patient may develop severe signs and symptoms very quickly. Signs of tension pneumothorax include distended neck veins, hypotension, severe shortness of breath, subcutaneous emphysema (air under the skin), and tracheal deviation to the side opposite the affected lung.

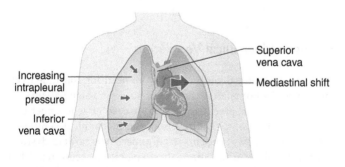

**FIGURE 10.3** Tension pneumothorax.

## Diagnostics

A pneumothorax is usually visible on a chest x-ray. When feasible, a chest x-ray should be taken if tension pneumothorax is suspected to determine size, severity, and involved structures.

## Intervention

If the patient already has a plural chest tube, patency should be maintained and it should be attached to –20 cm $H_2O$ wall suction. If the patient does not have a plural chest tube, one may be inserted by the physician if the pneumothorax is symptomatic. If the patient is experiencing a tension pneumothorax, a physician or other qualified provider should quickly decompress the affected lung with a 16-gauge needle placed in the second intercostal space at the midclavicular line.

▶ **NURSING IMPLICATIONS:** The cardiac surgery nurse should maintain the patency of chest tubes. Chest tubes may be gently milked if needed to keep them draining, but should not be stripped. Stripping chest tubes produces very high negative pressure in the chest cavity. Signs and symptoms of a pneumothorax should be recognized quickly. A chest x-ray will reveal a pneumothorax, if one exists, in a patient with acute shortness of breath.

## ESSENTIAL FACTS

Pneumothorax is a relatively rare complication that is usually resolved with a chest tube to relieve pressure.

## Prolonged Mechanical Ventilation

Prolonged mechanical ventilation is the need for continued ventilation past 24 hours after the end of surgery. Some patients, especially those with preexisting lung disease or who experience post-op complications, require prolonged mechanical ventilation after cardiac surgery. Patients who experience cardiac dysfunction, continual bleeding, surgical reexploration, acute renal failure, or need for blood transfusions are particularly at risk. The risk of prolonged mechanical ventilation is 1% to 5% (Coventry, 2014) and is associated with a higher mortality.

## Prevention

Optimizing cardiac function and hemodynamics, preventing other post-op complications, and intervening early when other post-op complications are present are the best ways to prevent prolonged mechanical ventilation.

## Assessment

These patients fail multiple attempts to wean from ventilation during the first 24 hours post-op. They often fail owing to problems with oxygenation, ventilation, or both.

## Diagnostics

Chest x-rays and arterial blood gas (ABG) readings may assist in determining a reason for failure to wean from the ventilator.

## Intervention

Patients who fail to wean after surgery require optimization of cardiac and volume status, correction of metabolic abnormalities, and initiation of nutrition (usually tube feedings). If a patient cannot be weaned from the ventilator after 10 to 14 days, a tracheostomy may be required. Patients requiring prolonged mechanical ventilation are at high risk for other complications, such as ventilator-associated pneumonia (VAP) and skin breakdown.

▶ **NURSING IMPLICATIONS:** Nurses play a large role in preventing complications in patients who require prolonged hospitalization. Prevention of infection from various sources, including skin breakdown, are important nursing functions. Nurses may also positively affect a patient's recovery by providing support to patients and families, including accurate information on patient progress, education about tests and procedures, and psychosocial support as required.

## ESSENTIAL FACTS

Patients who fail to wean and experience prolonged mechanical ventilation require astute nursing care to prevent other complications from arising.

# Pneumonia

Pneumonia is usually caused by a bacterial infection in the lungs and is more common in patients requiring mechanical ventilation for more than 48 hours and in those who develop dysfunction of the diaphragm after surgery. Patients are also at risk for developing pneumonia if they have incisional pain after surgery and do not effectively cough and deep breathe or if they have persistent left ventricular failure after surgery, resulting in fluid accumulation in the alveoli.

## Prevention

Care should be taken to prevent VAP in patients with prolonged mechanical ventilation. The VAP prevention bundle (a group of activities shown to reduce the incidence of VAP) includes keeping the head of the bed at 30 degrees or higher, daily interruption of sedation to assess for readiness for ventilator weaning and extubation, peptic ulcer prophylaxis, deep vein thrombosis prophylaxis, and daily oral care with 0.12% chlorhexidine gluconate (Zillberg, Shorr, & Kollef, 2009).

## Assessment

Patients who develop pneumonia frequently experience shortness of breath, decreased pulse oximetry readings, and fever. Lung sounds may be diminished or may be wet sounding.

## Diagnostics

Consolidation seen on a chest x-ray strongly suggests the presence of pneumonia and indicates the location and size of the infection. Sputum cultures taken either via sputum induction or bronchoscopy usually are positive.

## Intervention

Patients who develop bacterial pneumonia after cardiac surgery require antibiotics. Physician orders usually include initial administration of intravenous antibiotics with possible transition to oral antibiotics. Post-op pneumonia usually increases length of stay.

► **NURSING IMPLICATIONS:** Careful adherence to the VAP prevention bundle has been shown to decrease the incidence of VAP. Nurses play a large role in making sure these interventions are ordered and carried out.

*ESSENTIAL FACTS*

Routine oral care using 0.12% chlorhexidine gluconate in all post-op cardiac surgery patients has been shown to reduce the incidence of post-op VAP.

## Phrenic Nerve injury

The phrenic nerve enervates the diaphragm. Injury to this nerve may cause dysfunction of the diaphragm. This complication is rare, occurring in less than 0.5% of surgeries. The nerve may be injured by the use of iced slush (for cooling) in the pericardial cavity during surgery or during takedown of the internal mammary artery.

### Prevention

Many surgeons and surgical centers no longer use iced slush for cooling during cardiac surgery. Other methods of cooling, such as cold cardioplegia solution, allow for more control of temperature during surgery and do not lead to phrenic nerve injury. (See Chapter 4 for more details on cooling during surgery.)

### Assessment

If damage the phrenic nerve occurs on only one side, there may be few symptoms except for lower lobe atelectasis. If there is phrenic nerve injury on both sides, extubation may be difficult. During extubation, patients may experience paradoxical breathing, tachypnea, and carbon dioxide retention.

### Diagnostics

Chest x-ray may reveal an elevated hemidiaphragm at end expiration during spontaneous respiration. While the patient is being mechanically ventilated, elevated intrathoracic pressures prevent this from being seen on x-ray.

## Intervention

Plication of the diaphragm may be necessary to stabilize the muscle and prevent paradoxical movement with respiration. Plication is a generally successful surgical procedure during which excess diaphragmatic tissue is folded and sutured in place to tighten the diaphragm.

▶ **NURSING IMPLICATIONS:** The cardiac surgery nurse should be prepared to explain this complication and its treatment to patients and families.

## ESSENTIAL FACTS

Phrenic nerve injury is an uncommon complication of cardiac surgery that may lead to difficulty with extubation.

## Acute Lung Injury

Acute lung injury is uncommon after cardiac surgery, but patients who have had prior cardiac surgery, who experience shock, and who receive numerous blood products are at higher risk. Cardiopulmonary bypass may also play a role, as it stimulates a systemic inflammatory response. Lung injury caused by transfusion of blood products is called transfusion-related acute lung injury (TRALI).

**CLINICAL ALERT!** Acute respiratory distress syndrome (ARDS) is an extreme form of acute lung injury, characterized by leakage of fluid into the alveolar space, hypoxemia, and pulmonary infiltrates.

### Prevention

Carefully managing hemodynamic status post-op to prevent shock and minimizing the use of blood products may help in preventing some cases of acute lung injury.

### Assessment

Acute lung injury is characterized by very diminished or wet lung sounds, difficulty in maintaining oxygenation even with administration of high-flow oxygen, and inability to wean from the ventilator.

## Diagnostics

Patients with acute lung injury may have visible infiltrates on a chest x-ray. Patients with ARDS have a characteristic "whiteout" chest x-ray in which little lung tissue capable of exchanging oxygen is visible. An ABG is useful for determining level of oxygenation.

## Intervention

Acute lung injury, especially ARDS, is difficult to manage. Supportive treatment is given, and oxygenation is the primary goal. The use of small tidal volumes has been shown to prevent further lung damage and decrease mortality.

▶ **NURSING IMPLICATIONS:** Maintaining adequate oxygenation is the goal of treatment. The nurse should work with the physician and respiratory therapist to determine the best strategy for maintaining oxygenation in these patients. Usually this involves the use of low tidal volumes. ABGs are used to determine if treatment is working or if changes need to be made.

### ESSENTIAL FACTS

Acute lung injury is an uncommon but serious complication after cardiac surgery. It may occur as a result of a systemic inflammatory response to cardiopulmonary bypass or multiple blood transfusions.

### ESSENTIAL FACTS

Prolonged hypotension and decreased CO may cause ischemia to multiple organ systems in the body. Maintaining post-op CO at a level where perfusion is adequate is a primary nursing goal to prevent multiple complications. Prevention of pulmonary complications is also critical during the initial post-op period.

# REFERENCES

Coventry, B. J. (Ed.). (2014). *Cardio-thoracic, vascular, renal and transplant surgery*. London, UK: Springer.

Hillis, L. D., Smith, P. K., Anderson, J. L., Bittl, J. A., Bridges C. R., Byrne J. G., . . . Winniford, M. D. (2011). 2011 ACCF/AHA guideline for coronary artery bypass graft surgery: A report of the American College of Cardiology Foundation/American Heart Association Task Force on Practice Guidelines. *Journal of the American College of Cardiology, 48,* e123–e210.

Jacobson, C., Marzlin, K., & Webner, C. (2007). *Cardiovascular nursing practice*. Burien, WA: Cardiovascular Nursing Education Associates.

Zillberg, M. D., Shorr, A. F., & Kollef, M. H., (2009). Implementing quality improvements in the intensive care unit: Ventilator bundle as an example. *Critical Care Medicine, 37*(1), 305–309.

# BIBLIOGRAPHY

Bojar, R. M. (2011). *Manual of perioperative care in adult cardiac surgery* (5th ed.). West Sussex, UK: Wiley-Blackwell.

DeRiso, A. J., II, Ladowski, J. S., Dillon, T. A., Justice, J. W., & Peterson, A. C. (1996). Chlorhexidine gluconate 0.12% oral rinse reduces the incidence of total nosocomial respiratory infection and nonprophylactic systemic antibiotic use in patients undergoing heart surgery. *Chest, 109,* 1556–1561.

Hardin, S. R., & Kaplow, R. (Eds.). (2010). *Cardiac surgery essentials for critical care nursing*. Sudbury, MA: Jones & Bartlett.

Munro, C. L., Grap, M. J., Jones, D. J., McClish, D. K., & Sessler, C. N. (2009). Chlorhexidine, toothbrushing, and preventing ventilator-associated pneumonia in critically ill adults. *American Journal of Critical Care, 18,* 428–437.

Steiner, M. E., & Despotis, G. J. (2007). Transfusion algorithms and how they apply to blood conservation: The high-risk cardiac surgical patient. *Hematology/Oncology Clinics of North America, 21,* 177–184.

Versteegh, M. I. M., & Tjien, A. T. J. (2007). Diaphragm plication in adult patients with diaphragm paralysis. *Multimedia manual of cardiothoracic surgery.* doi:10.1510/mmcts.2006.002568

# Transition to Intermediate Care

*Once patients have initially recovered from cardiac surgery in the intensive care unit (ICU), they are usually transferred to an acute care or step-down unit until discharge. Throughout this chapter, these types of units will be referred to as intermediate care units. This transition is a critical step in the recovery process. There are many pitfalls possible in this process, including breakdowns in communication, rushed transfers, and lack of comprehensive discharge planning. Collaboration is critical in successfully transferring patients.*

## Objectives

In this chapter, you will learn:

1. How to prepare patients for transfer out of the ICU
2. Key information that must be communicated upon transfer
3. Steps to take to ensure transfer is as smooth as possible

## PATIENT READINESS FOR TRANSFER

Patients should not be transferred out of the ICU until they are hemodynamically stable enough for a lower level of care. Each intermediate care unit has its own admission criteria depending on staffing levels and the training and expertise of the nurses on the unit. Typically, these requirements include a stable respiratory status and blood pressure and the absence of intravenous medications required to support blood pressure or cardiac output. Chest tubes and epicardial pacing wires may or may not be removed prior to transfer from the ICU.

## Cardiovascular Status

A pulmonary artery catheter must be removed prior to transfer from the ICU. Patients who still need cardiac output readings, pulmonary artery pressures, or other measurements gathered using a pulmonary artery catheter also still require ICU care. In general, arterial lines must be removed, although some intermediate care units have the capability of caring for patients with these lines. Typically, patients should be stable on oral medications before transfer. Some patients may require low doses of certain vasoactive medications (e.g., dopamine at 5 mcg/kg/min or less) or other intravenous medications that require little titration.

Cardiac surgery patients require continuous electrocardiographic (ECG) monitoring. On an intermediate care unit, this typically involves a telemetry monitor. After cardiac surgery, patients are at high risk for the development of atrial fibrillation or other arrhythmias. Atrial fibrillation often develops around postoperative day (POD) 3. Typically, epicardial pacing wires remain in place until about POD 4. At that point, if they are not needed they will be removed. If patients have experienced bradycardia, heart blocks, ventricular arrhythmias, or atrial fibrillation requiring intravenous amiodarone, pacing wires may remain in place longer in case they are needed.

Vital signs and assessments are performed less frequently on an intermediate care unit than in the ICU. Vital signs may be assessed every 2 hours if required, but usually every 4 hours is routine. Physical assessments typically occur every 4 hours.

## Respiratory Status

Patients transferred to an intermediate care unit should have a stable respiratory status. They often require oxygen therapy but should not be in distress when transferred. On transfer out of ICU, chest tubes may remain in place if drainage is stable, a pleural effusion remains, or there is an air leak. Chest tube output is typically monitored less frequently than in an ICU.

If required, some intermediate care units will accept patients who need continuous positive airway pressure (CPAP) or bilevel positive airway pressure (BiPAP). Some units are trained and staffed to care for patients who are stable on a mechanical ventilator. These patients must have an established tracheostomy prior to transfer. Patients with an endotracheal tube require ICU care.

## Neurological Status

Many cardiac surgery patients experience neurological complications after surgery (see Chapters 13 and 14 for more information). Patients should not be transferred to intermediate care during the acute phase of a stroke. However, many patients are transferred while still confused or otherwise neurologically impaired. These patients often require very close monitoring to maintain their safety. Staffing levels and the ability of the intermediate care unit to closely monitor these patients should be taken into account prior to transfer.

▶ **NURSING IMPLICATIONS:** It is the responsibility of nurses, both in the ICU and on an intermediate care unit, to advocate for patients if their stability and readiness for transfer are in question. If a transfer must take place, the patient should be assigned to an experienced nurse on the intermediate care unit or, if assigned to an inexperienced nurse, assistance should be made available to ensure appropriate care for the patient. See the section "Special Circumstances" later in this chapter for a discussion about transferring patients who may not be quite ready for transfer.

### *ESSENTIAL FACTS*

Patients need to be stable upon transfer from ICU to an intermediate care unit. The receiving unit must have the knowledge and skills to care for a patient who is transferred.

# PATIENT AND FAMILY EDUCATION

It is important that patients and families are prepared for transfer out of ICU to a lower level of care. Some patients and their families are very anxious about leaving the security of the ICU. This is especially true if complications have been experienced or the ICU stay has been prolonged. Having a nurse in sight at all times can be very comforting for some people. The highly technological character of the ICU, while initially overwhelming, may provide comfort and security to patients and families. A move to another unit where staff are not known and monitoring equipment is not readily apparent can be frightening. This phenomenon has been called transfer anxiety.

Patients and families are often unprepared for the change in staffing ratios and have feelings of abandonment. They may have unrealistic expectations of care in the intermediate care unit, which can create feelings of insecurity and mistrust. These problems are created and exacerbated by a lack of communication between ICU and intermediate care nurses and a rushed transfer process, which lead to a lack of adequate preparation for transfer. If resources in the intermediate care unit are inadequate (staffing, knowledge, and clinical skills to care for high-acuity patients), this may compound the problem.

## *ESSENTIAL FACTS*

To avoid transfer anxiety, patients and families should be given a realistic idea of what to expect on the intermediate care unit. Communication between the ICU and intermediate care unit is critical to adequately prepare patients and families for transfer.

## Preparing for a Lower Level of Care

The transition to intermediate care is made less stressful for patients and families when they have realistic information about what to expect. This is often difficult for ICU nurses, who may not be completely familiar with the routines on the intermediate care floor. It is important that ICU nurses become familiar with the intermediate care units where their patients will be sent, so they can adequately educate patients and families prior to transfer. If written information is available, this should be used as well.

Several strategies have been developed to aid in the transfer process and help alleviate anxiety that patients and families may feel. The ICU should be presented as a temporary accommodation, with transfer to intermediate care as a sign of progress and healing. It is important for patients and families to talk about the intermediate care unit and the nurses on that unit in a positive light. ICU nurses should never criticize the knowledge, skills, or staffing levels in the intermediate care unit; if patients or families overhear, it will erode their confidence and create more anxiety upon transfer. Whenever possible, patients and families should be informed of the plan to transfer and should be involved in the planning process. Unless absolutely necessary, transfers to intermediate care should occur during the daytime, when resources are more plentiful, staffing is often better, and families can participate. Patients and families should be encouraged to ask questions and should be kept up to date on medical progress.

▶ **NURSING IMPLICATIONS:** A smooth transition between units requires a good working relationship and effective communication between nurses in the ICU and in the intermediate care unit. In addition, patients and families should be prepared for transfer through education on realistic expectations for the intermediate care unit. These strategies decrease the anxiety experienced by patients and families and may ultimately reduce complications.

## *ESSENTIAL FACTS*

Transfer to an intermediate care unit should be presented as evidence of patient progress and healing.

## Hand-Off Communication

Often, intermediate care nurses have anxiety about receiving patients from the ICU. These patients tend to require more care and have a greater tendency for complications than those who have been on the intermediate care unit for several days. Good rapport between ICU and intermediate care nurses is important to alleviate anxiety felt by nurses and improve communication. A collaborative relationship makes for the smoothest transition and is best for the patient. If an intermediate care nurse is intimidated by an ICU nurse, which is often the case when nurses are new or inexperienced, this response can prevent the nurse from asking important questions and may lead the nurse to miss or misunderstand information about the patient's care. ICU nurses sometimes feel that intermediate care nurses are less qualified or skilled than those who manage acute care problems. This attitude can also hamper important communication.

There is a difference in environment and culture between the ICU and intermediate care unit. Care in the ICU is much more focused on technology and patient monitoring. In intermediate care, these activities makes up a much smaller portion of patient care. Intermediate care nurses are more focused on education, assisting patients to be more self-sufficient, and moving patients toward discharge. Their patients are not as acutely sick but there are more of them. Physicians may not be as readily available in intermediate care as they are in the ICU. If the patient transfer process includes having the intermediate care nurse go to the ICU, the differences in environment can be very intimidating.

There is also often a difference in communication style between ICU nurses and intermediate care nurses. ICU nurses may tend to communicate everything about the patient's stay and all the details about what happened in the ICU. From the perspective of the intermediate care nurses, this is often too much detail and makes for an unnecessarily lengthy report. Also, ICU nurses are more likely to have a medical focus when giving report. Intermediate care nurses are often more focused on the patient's abilities (e.g., activity level, diet, and ability to feed themselves).

For these reasons, collaboration between ICU and intermediate care nurses can be difficult. Collaboration is more likely to occur when patients have obvious special needs, such as a need for specialized equipment that must be arranged ahead of time. Collaboration also is more common if patients might be likely to be readmitted to the ICU due to complications after cardiac surgery, since ICU nurses may be more worried and protective of these patients. If a patient will be transferred with a device, procedure, or medication with which intermediate care nurses are unfamiliar, ICU nurses often spend more time communicating information about the patient.

Collaboration between nurses in the ICU and intermediate care unit is essential for a smooth patient transition between the two units.

## Information That Must Be Communicated

Communication is critical for patient care and maintaining patient safety. The period during which hand-off communication or shift report occurs is a critical and vulnerable point in a patient's hospital stay. It is during this period that information can be and often is omitted and distorted, providing an opportunity for error to occur. This is especially true when a patient is being transferred from one unit to another, since nurses in the receiving unit do not know the patient. Communication between care providers is such an important issue that The Joint Commission has made it a requirement that hospitals have a standard communication format and that adequate time be allotted for asking and answering questions. One such format is SBAR (Situation, Background, Assessment, Recommendation). Some elements that are known to improve hand-off communication include a face-to-face verbal report with opportunity for questions, limited interruptions, presentation of information in the same order every time, read-back by the receiving nurse to ensure comprehension, and review of the current status and historical data by the receiving nurse.

For a smooth transition, patient needs and routines should be communicated. Physician orders should remain consistent between ICU and intermediate care whenever possible. Physician orders and patient medications should be reviewed, including what medications have already been given on the day of transfer. Miscommunication about medication administration can lead to medication errors by over or under dosing of medications. (See Table 11.1 for an example of information that should be included in a transfer report.)

▶ **NURSING IMPLICATIONS:** Hand-off communication is a critical component of patient care. The standard format used at an institution for hand-off communication should be used every time a patient is transferred. Cardiac surgery nurses should ask questions

### TABLE 11.1 Critical Information on Transfer From ICU to Intermediate Care

| Procedures, Complications, and Orders | Physical and Psychosocial Recovery | Family and Other Issues |
|---|---|---|
| Surgical procedure performed | Physical assessment findings | Family presence and interactions with patient |
| Any additional procedures performed in the ICU or operating room | Activity level in the ICU | |
| | Level of pain, pain medication last administered | Family's level of anxiety |
| Complications experienced | Incentive spirometer reading | Any problems experienced with family members |
| Physician orders | Required procedures (e.g., dressing changes) and when next procedure is due | Who will care for patient at home |
| Medications administered | | |
| | Psychosocial factors (e.g., depressed, anxious, refusal to participate in care) | |

about anything that needs to be clarified. These questions must be answered appropriately. Animosity between caregivers and intimidation hamper the flow of information and can negatively impact a patient's recovery.

## ESSENTIAL FACTS

Hand-off communication is critical to prevent medical errors and improve patient safety. A consistent approach to giving report and allowing opportunity for questions are important for improving hand-off communication.

## SPECIAL CIRCUMSTANCES

### Urgent Transfer to Make a Bed

The decision to transfer a patient from the ICU to an intermediate care unit involves both patient readiness and the availability of hospital beds. Patient transfers that are done hurriedly, when the need for an ICU bed is urgent, may cause stress for all parties involved (ICU and intermediate care nurses, patients, and families). It is not uncommon for nurses to delay or slow a patient transfer when they feel that the patient is not ready for a lower level of care. However, this can be problematic for patient flow in the hospital.

There is evidence in the literature that patients are sometimes transferred to a lower level of care before they are ready because of shortages of ICU beds. This creates a risk of readmission to the ICU if the intermediate care unit is not properly equipped to care for these patients (i.e., because of inadequate staffing, knowledge, or ability to care for certain acute patients). There is also a risk that preventable complications may occur or that complications may not be identified in a timely manner. If this is an ongoing issue, unit management or hospital administration may need to assist in finding a solution that is safe for patients and acceptable to the flow of patients in the hospital. Strategies may include providing additional resources and education for the intermediate care unit.

▶ **NURSING IMPLICATIONS:** If, on a regular basis, patients are transferred because of ICU bed shortages rather than patient readiness for transfer, cardiac surgery nurses should work with managers and administrators to identify strategies to keep patients safe while meeting the needs of the hospital.

## Transfer to a Long-Term Facility From the ICU

Not every patient is transferred from the ICU to an intermediate care unit. In some situations, such as for insurance reasons, patients may be transferred from the ICU to another hospital. Another trend is to transfer long-term patients, who typically have experienced multiple complications and are debilitated, to a long-term facility. These facilities are designed to care for critical or acute care patients for a month or more. Staff at these facilities are specially trained in caring for these patients and are usually specialists in ventilator weaning, progressive mobility, and rehabilitation.

When sending cardiac surgery patients to another facility, it is critical that all medical records are copied and sent and that a thorough verbal report is given. The nurses at the receiving facility may not be familiar with caring for patients after cardiac surgery. Topics specific to cardiac surgery patients, such as incision care and activity restrictions, should be reviewed. If possible, written information should be sent to the receiving facility on these topics.

## ICU Liaison Nurse

Some hospitals employ an ICU liaison nurse to assist with the transition from ICU to intermediate care. Typically, this is a nurse with ICU experience who works with ICU and intermediate care nurses to ease the transition between levels of care. This role may also be fulfilled by a discharge planning nurse or an advanced practice nurse (clinical nurse specialist, clinical nurse leader, or nurse practitioner). Someone in this position is uniquely qualified to educate the patient and family and influence their perception of the transfer. A liaison nurse can also support and educate the intermediate care nurses about very acute patients or new devices, medications, or procedures.

## *ESSENTIAL FACTS*

Not every patient transfer is routine. Some patients are transferred hurriedly and possibly before they are ready. Transfers may also occur to other facilities. Appropriate hand-off communication is even more vital in these situations.

## BIBLIOGRAPHY

Chaboyer, W., James, H., & Kendall, M. (2005). Transitional care after the intensive care unit: Current trends and future directions. *Critical Care Nurse, 25*, 16–28.

Dracup, K., & Morris, P. E. (2008). Passing the torch: The challenge of handoffs. *American journal of critical care, 17*, 95–97.

Haggstrom, M., Asplund, K., & Kristiansen, L. (2009). Struggle with a gap between intensive care units and general wards. *International Journal of Qualitative Studies on Health and Well-Being, 4*, 181–192.

Haig, K. M., Sutton, S., & Whittington, J. (2006). SBAR: A shared mental model for improving communication between clinicians. *Joint Commission Journal on Quality and Patient Safety, 32*(3), 167–175.

PART

# IV

# Extended Postoperative Period

VI

Extending the Scope of Practice

# 12

## Extended Recovery Timelines

*There is increasing pressure to send patients home as soon as possible after cardiac surgery. Most institutions have specific timelines or collaborative pathways that uncomplicated patients are expected to follow. Once patients transfer out of the intensive care unit (ICU) to an intermediate care unit, they are expected to move steadily toward discharge. Nurses need to be aware of what care individual patients need to move them toward these goals. Nurses are in a unique position to influence progress toward a speedy discharge.*

### Objectives

In this chapter, you will learn:

1. Goals patients need to achieve prior to discharge
2. Timelines for meeting goals for discharge

## GOALS FOR RECOVERY

After cardiac surgery, most patients are transferred out of the ICU on postoperative day (POD) 1 or 2. The actual time of transfer depends on the time of day when surgery was completed and how quickly the patient was extubated and became hemodynamically stable. Patients who do not experience serious complications after surgery should approximately follow the timeline discussed below. Some patients are slower to progress along the expected recovery pathway. These include the very elderly and patients with preoperative comorbidities such as respiratory disease, diabetes, obesity, renal failure, myocardial infarction (MI), cardiac arrest, or cardiogenic shock.

## CARDIOVASCULAR

One of the main goals after cardiac surgery is a stable cardiovascular status. The uncomplicated patient should be hemodynamically stable and weaned off vasoactive medications by POD 1. Once stable, the pulmonary artery catheter and any arterial lines may be discontinued. A central line should be left in place while the patient is receiving intravenous (IV) medications that may damage peripheral vessels. In patients for whom a central line is no longer needed, a peripheral IV line should be placed prior to removal of the central line. IV access should be maintained until discharge.

▶ **NURSING IMPLICATIONS:** Nurses play an important role in making sure invasive lines are removed when no longer needed. If no orders exist to remove the pulmonary artery catheter or arterial line or to place a peripheral IV and discontinue the central line, orders should be obtained from the physician.

## *ESSENTIAL FACTS*

Invasive monitoring catheters and central lines should be removed as soon as possible to prevent catheter related bloodstream infection.

Once transferred to intermediate care, cardiac surgery patients should be monitored using telemetry, because they are at very high risk of arrhythmias during the period after surgery. Once transferred, vital signs should be monitored every 4 to 8 hours until discharge.

# Medications

Aspirin should be started 6 to 8 hours postoperatively. If the patient is unable to take aspirin orally, aspirin should be given via nasogastric (NG) tube, or as a suppository. Aspirin should be held in patients with a platelet count less than 100,000 mm$^3$. A beta-blocker should be started as soon as the patient is hemodynamically stable and the blood pressure and heart rate will tolerate it (typically systolic blood pressure over 90–100 mmHg and heart rate greater than 50–55 beats per minute). Serum potassium should be kept at or above 4 to 5 mg/dL and serum magnesium at or above 2 mg/dL.

▶ **NURSING IMPLICATIONS:** Administration of medications per physician order is critical in cardiac surgery patients to prevent complications. Aspirin is given to improve graft patency and prevent thromboembolism from implanted valves after surgery. Beta-blockers reduce the incidence of perioperative MI and may help prevent atrial fibrillation and other arrhythmias. Maintaining serum potassium and magnesium at ordered levels is important for prevention of arrhythmias.

## Epicardial Wires

Once a patient's rhythm is stable and a pacemaker is no longer needed, epicardial pacing wires should be electrically isolated and taped to the patient's chest. Care should be taken not to touch the end of these wires with bare hands. Static electrical energy could be transmitted down the wire directly to the patient's heart. Wires should be taped in place so they are not inadvertently pulled out.

### ESSENTIAL FACTS

When not in use, epicardial pacing wires should be electrically isolated to prevent electrical shock to the heart. However, wires should be easily and quickly accessible in case pacing is emergently required.

Epicardial pacing wires should be removed on POD 4 or 5 if not being used to pace the patient and if the patient's rhythm has been stable for at least 24 hours. Epicardial pacing wires must be removed prior to discharge. These wires may be removed by a physician or other specially trained health care provider. They are usually removed by pulling straight out and applying pressure to the insertion site. Patients should be on bed rest for 1 hour after epicardial wire removal and should be monitored for signs of cardiac tamponade for several hours after removal.

▶ **NURSING IMPLICATIONS:** Epicardial pacing wires must be managed appropriately to avoid complications. They must be electrically isolated and taped to avoid accidental dislodgement. After removal, patients must be monitored for signs and symptoms of cardiac tamponade. (See Chapter 10 for more information on cardiac tamponade.)

## RESPIRATORY

Patients should be weaned from the ventilator and extubated within 4 to 12 hours after surgery. Once extubated, patients usually require low-flow oxygen for a few days. Oxygen saturation should be kept greater than 92%. Oxygen should be weaned off prior to discharge unless the patient was oxygen dependent prior to surgery. Patients should use an incentive spirometer every hour while awake. This is critical for resolution of postoperative atelectasis. They should also be encouraged to cough to clear any respiratory secretions. Patients will need to splint the midline sternotomy incision by wrapping their arms around a pillow and holding it tightly to their chest while coughing. This stabilizes the incision and decreases pain involved in coughing and taking deep breaths.

▶ **NURSING IMPLICATIONS:** Patients need to be educated and encouraged to cough, deep breathe, and use an incentive spirometer every hour. Family members should be educated and enlisted, whenever possible, to assist in reminding patients to perform these important respiratory exercises. Patients and families should be taught that these exercises and ambulation are the two most important things they can do to speed recovery and reduce complications.

Coughing, deep breathing, and incentive spirometry are all important for lung expansion and improving postoperative atelectasis.

## FLUID STATUS

Immediately after surgery, intake and output should be measured every hour. Urine output should be kept greater than 0.5 mL/kg/hr. Weight should be monitored daily and compared with preoperative weight. Edema and fluid retention after cardiac surgery are common. Diuretics, especially furosemide (Lasix), are often used to help rid the body of excess fluid. Edema hampers healing of incisions and the goal is to return patients to their preoperative weight.

*ESSENTIAL FACTS*

Diuretics are commonly used to decrease edema and help patients return to their preoperative weight. This is important for wound healing.

## WOUNDS AND DRAINS

Assessing surgical wounds and drains is important for preventing and catching early signs and symptoms of infection. Prophylactic antibiotics are given just before surgery (within an hour of cut time) and continued for 24 to 48 hours. Unless there is an indication of infection, antibiotics should not be given for more than 48 hours after surgery. Signs and symptoms of infection include redness at the incision site, incisional pain or tenderness (especially if pain is worsening), drainage from the incision, and fever or malaise.

▶ **NURSING IMPLICATIONS:** Patients should be educated on the signs and symptoms of infection. They will need to know this information upon discharge. They also need to know what to report to the nurse or physician while in the hospital.

# Drains

Patients typically come out of the operating room with a urinary catheter and one or more chest tubes. To reduce the risk
of a catheter-related urinary tract infection, the urinary catheter
should be removed no later than POD 2 unless there is an appropriate indication to leave it in place. According to the Centers for
Disease Control, in its campaign to reduce hospital-acquired infections, a urinary catheter may be left in place after POD 2:

- If the patient has acute urinary retention or bladder outlet
  obstruction
- If there is a need for accurate measures of urinary output in
  critically ill patients
- If there is a need to assist in healing of open sacral or perineal
  wounds in incontinent patients
- If the patient requires prolonged immobilization
- To improve comfort for end of life care if needed

Chest tubes may be removed per physician's order when drainage is less than 100 to 150 mL in an 8-hour period with no air leak.
Once chest tubes are removed, a sterile dressing should be maintained over the chest tube site for 48 hours. After this period, chest
tube sites should be monitored every shift for signs of infection.

## Midline Sternotomy Incisions

An infected surgical incision can be very serious. A midline sternotomy incision can be especially problematic if it becomes infected. Several steps can be taken to maintain the stability of the
sternal incision, which may help to prevent infection. Patients
should be given restrictions on how much weight they may lift and
how they use their arms to lift themselves. These restrictions are
often called sternal precautions. (See Table 12.1 for an example of
sternal precautions.)

A midline sternotomy incision can be especially problematic for
large-breasted women. The downward and lateral pull of breasts
on the incision can lead to increased pain, slower healing, and
increased risk of infection. Women who wear a B-cup or larger-sized
bra may be more comfortable postoperatively and have less risk of
infection if they wear a supportive bra. A bra that closes in the front
and does not rub against the incision is the best. A bra that closes

**TABLE 12.1  Sternal Precautions: Patient Instructions**

- Do not lift, push, or pull more than 10 pounds
- Avoid extremes of reaching with your arms for 1 month (Do not raise your elbows higher than your shoulders. Do not reach behind you.)
- Do not let people pull on your arms when they are helping you move
- To stand, use your leg muscles to push yourself up, and your arms only to guide you for balance
- To move from a lying to sitting position, roll over onto your side and use your elbows to push up
- If you hear popping or clicking from your sternum, tell your nurse or doctor

in the back can be worn if someone is available to assist, because reaching both arms to the back to clasp the bra can place tension on the incision. If possible, large-breasted women should be instructed, prior to surgery, to bring such a bra to the hospital. Small-breasted women (less than a B-cup size) who wear a bra after surgery often have increased pain without a decrease in risk for sternal infection.

▶ **NURSING IMPLICATIONS:** Education on sternal precautions accompanied by constant reinforcement is important, because patients frequently forget and try to reach and push with their arms. Family members should also receive this instruction so they can help in reinforcing sternal precautions, both in the hospital and at home.

*ESSENTIAL FACTS*

Following sternal precautions and requesting all large-breasted women to wear a bra after surgery can decrease the risk of sternal infections.

## Caring for Incisions

Proper care of surgical incisions and education for patients and families about how to care for incisions at home are crucial for preventing infection. Immediately after surgery, surgical incisions should be covered with sterile dressings. Sterile dressings should be maintained over incisions for 48 to 72 hours after surgery. After this period of time, incisions should be left open to air unless there is drainage from the incision. Once the sterile dressings are removed, incisions should be washed daily. Depending on the institution's policy and surgeon's preference, incisions are either washed with a gentle soap and water to remove debris and any bacteria that might be present or cleansed with an antibacterial solution (povidone–iodine or chlorhexidine). Either way, patients should be instructed on how to cleanse their own incisions in preparation for discharge.

Edema in the extremities where there are incisions can delay wound healing. Affected extremities may be wrapped with an elasticized bandage immediately after surgery to help reduce edema. Extremities wrapped in such a manner must be monitored closely for adequate circulation. Circulation, sensation, and movement should be assessed at least every few hours. At least once a shift, the wrap should be removed to check the underlying skin for areas of excessive pressure. If the extremity is to be rewrapped, the bandage should be wrapped distal to proximal. Once the patient is mobile and getting out of bed, edematous extremities should be kept elevated to minimize edema and stress on the incisions.

▶ **NURSING IMPLICATIONS:** By the time of discharge, patients and family members should know how to care for incisions at home. The patient or a family member should perform incision care with supervision and should be independent with care by discharge. Edematous extremities should be elevated while patients are in the hospital, and patients should be instructed to do so at home.

## *ESSENTIAL FACTS*

Proper incisional care and minimizing edema can improve healing and reduce the risk of infection.

## PAIN CONTROL

Uncontrolled pain prevents patients from taking deep breaths and from engaging in increasing activity, which can lead to inadequate progression toward goals. Pain medication should be given to keep patients comfortable. Immediately after surgery, IV pain medications should be used. Typically, narcotic pain medication is used (morphine, dilaudid, or fentanyl). This may be given through a patient-controlled device or on an as-needed basis. A nonsteroidal anti-inflammatory agent (NSAID), such as ketorolac (Toradol) may be used as well. If used, NSAIDs must be limited to no longer than 72 hours of use and cannot be used if there are kidney problems or bleeding issues. Once patients are eating, oral pain medication should be started. Combination agents (acetaminophen [Tylenol] with a narcotic agent) are typically used. IV narcotic agents may be given for breakthrough pain.

Adequate pain assessment is crucial, and patients should be closely involved in this process. The most reliable indicator of a patient's pain level is a stated report. Each patient should be asked about an acceptable level of pain based on the pain scale being used. Every effort should be made to keep the level of pain at or below that individual patient's stated goal.

Some patients, especially the elderly, resist taking pain medication. Sometimes this is due to fear of addiction or of side effects. They may be comfortable while lying still, but have excessive pain while moving. This scenario hampers the healing process. Patients should be educated about the importance of pain control in the context of increasing activity levels and deep breathing for healing and recovery.

Other patients seem to require a lot of pain medication. This may be due to tolerance if patients take opioid pain medication at home for chronic pain. It could also be due to a higher innate tolerance or faster than normal metabolism of the medication. Patients who state they are in pain should be treated for pain. Patients who are thought to be "drug-seeking" may not get adequate medication for pain and may have a more difficult recovery. If pain management is a problem, an expert in pain management should be consulted, if possible.

▶ **NURSING IMPLICATIONS:** The bedside nurse plays a critical role in pain management. Proper pain management includes a thorough pain assessment and evaluation of response to treatments for pain. The goal is not to eliminate all pain, but to allow patients to move and breathe to prevent complications of surgery. A patient's pain is whatever he or she says it is.

## ESSENTIAL FACTS

Managing pain, usually with narcotic pain medications, is important for the recovery process and allows patients to move and breathe deeply as needed.

# NUTRITION AND GASTROINTESTINAL CARE

Prior to and immediately after surgery, patients are kept NPO. While intubated, patients typically have a NG or an orogastric (OG) tube in place. Once they are extubated, the NG or OG tube may be removed and they may be started on a clear liquid diet. Diet is typically advanced as tolerated, and by POD 2 or 3 most patients are taking solid foods. Diet should be individualized for the patient, but most patients are allowed a low-sodium diet. If the patient is diabetic, a low-sodium, controlled carbohydrate diet should be given. Other restrictions may be required or requested (renal diet if kidney problems exist; vegetarian, kosher, or other restrictions as requested by the patient).

It is common for patients to have a poor appetite after surgery. Attempts should be made to find foods the patient feels like eating. Typically, these are lighter density foods. Patients should be encouraged to eat as much as they can, but should be told that loss of appetite is normal after surgery. Due to poor appetite, some surgeons prefer that diet not be restricted until appetite returns in several weeks.

## Bowel Care

Many medications given during the perioperative period slow down the gastrointestinal tract. Anesthetics and narcotics are the main culprits. It is important to ensure that the bowel is working prior to discharging a patient. Bowel care, including the administration of stool softeners and laxatives, is often needed. Stool softeners should be started as soon as the patient is extubated and taking oral medications. Starting on POD 2, patients should be assessed for bowel functioning. Progressively stronger laxatives may be given per physician's order over the next few days until results are seen. For example, patients may be started with prune juice, psyllium (Metamucil), or magnesium hydroxide (milk of magnesia). If there are no results, a laxative suppository may be given. An enema may be used as a final attempt to induce a bowel movement.

▶ **NURSING IMPLICATIONS:** Bowel care is often ordered on an as-needed basis. It is up to the nurse to ask about bowel movements and administer laxative agents per physician's order. This should be done early in the hospital stay, before the patient is uncomfortable and asks for a laxative.

Upon discharge, patients should be eating and have bowel function. Progressive bowel care should be started early to ensure patients have a bowel movement prior to discharge.

## Glucose Control

Keeping blood glucose under control is critical for recovery. Hyperglycemia after cardiac surgery increases mortality, sternal infection rates, and other complications. Keeping blood glucose under control for at least the first 3 PODs decreases these risks. The best range in which to keep blood glucose is currently under debate, and research is ongoing to find the optimum target blood glucose. However, for a patient with a blood glucose level greater than 180 mg/dL in the first few PODs, an insulin infusion may be warranted.

## ACTIVITY

Recovery from cardiac surgery requires a progressive mix of activity and rest. Each day, patients should be increasing their time out of bed, and walking duration and frequency. Once extubated, patients should be helped out of bed to a chair. On POD 1, they should be up to sitting in a chair three times a day. By POD 2, as they transition to intermediate care, patients should ambulate in their room three times a day and work toward ambulation in the hallway four times a day. Patients require assistance at first, but as they gain strength and stability, they should be able to ambulate without assistance. By discharge, patients should be ambulating in the hallway at least four times a day. If possible, patients should be given the opportunity to climb stairs with assistance prior to discharge.

▶ **NURSING IMPLICATIONS:** The cardiac surgery nurse is pivotal in encouraging patients to increase activity, in assisting them to ambulate, and in educating patients and families about the importance of ambulation in the recovery process.

## ESSENTIAL FACTS

Progressively increasing activity until patients are ambulating in the hallway at least four times a day is important for the recovery process.

## TESTS AND LABS

After cardiac surgery, it is important to regularly test blood counts and serum chemistries. Immediately after surgery, a complete blood count (CBC), complete metabolic (chemistry) panel, arterial blood gases, prothrombin time/international normalized ratio (PT/INR), partial thromboplastin time (PTT), chest x-ray, and 12-lead electrocardiogram (ECG) should be taken, per physician's orders. If bleeding is suspected, CBC, PT/INR, and PTT should be redrawn as ordered. Serum potassium and magnesium levels should be ordered and drawn regularly to ensure they are within the ordered range. Once patients are hemodynamically stable, chemistries and CBC should be ordered daily. PT/INR should be ordered daily if patients are taking warfarin (Coumadin). A chest x-ray should be completed daily while the patient is intubated or if chest tubes are in place. A chest x-ray should be ordered after chest tube removal. Prior to discharge, a 12-lead ECG should be completed in addition to the daily labs. Patients who have undergone valve replacement often have an echocardiogram completed prior to discharge to evaluate functioning of the new valve.

## ANTICOAGULATION

Some cardiac surgery patients require anticoagulation prior to discharge from the hospital. This includes all patients who received a mechanical valve, some patients who received a tissue valve (short term), and patients in persistent or permanent atrial fibrillation. Patients who require anticoagulation usually start taking warfarin (Coumadin) on POD 1 or 2 and will need to have a therapeutic PT/INR prior to discharge. The therapeutic range depends on the indication but is usually an INR of 2 to 3 for atrial fibrillation and most valves and an INR of 2.5 to 3.5 for some mechanical valves. There are several new oral anticoagulants, but none have been studied in cardiac surgery patients. Until there is more evidence or familiarity with use, most cardiac surgery patients requiring anticoagulation will be given warfarin.

## DISCHARGE PLANNING

Discharge planning is an important part of the recovery process and should begin early. Ideally, an assessment of the home environment (family or caregivers, stairs, adequate food, etc.) will take place prior to surgery on admission. Once patients reach the intermediate care floor, an assessment should be made to determine what, if any, medical supplies will be needed upon discharge. Also, if special services, such as home care or skilled nursing care, will be needed, this should be determined as early as possible so arrangements can be made.

▶ **NURSING IMPLICATIONS:** The bedside nurse should work with discharge planners and case managers to determine needs upon discharge and make arrangements to meet those needs. Family members should also be involved in this process.

## TEACHING

Patient and family education is one of the most important aspects of preparing a patient for discharge and should not wait until the day of discharge. Every day during a patient's stay, patients and families should be educated on medications, progress toward discharge, pain control and pain medications, expectations for activity levels, sternal precautions, caring for incisions, signs and symptoms of infection, and diet. Patients should participate in their own care as much as they are able. Because patients retain only a fraction of what they are taught while in the hospital, repetition is important for learning. Families should be involved when possible, especially family members who will be caring for patients at home. If available, patients should receive written materials on discharge outlining requirements for home care. Patients and families should also attend a discharge class or view a discharge video about home care. (Discharge education will be discussed in more detail in Chapter 15.)

▶ **NURSING IMPLICATIONS:** Patient education is a nursing responsibility and should occur throughout the hospital stay. A teaching record should be available to all caregivers so education can be seamless and each caregiver can start where the last one left off.

## ESSENTIAL FACTS

Nurses play a pivotal role in a patient's recovery from cardiac surgery. Monitoring for complications and performing activities to prevent complications are central to this role. Encouraging deep breathing, working with a patient to increase activity, and educating patients and families on self-care are some of the most important ways to prevent complications in these patients.

## BIBLIOGRAPHY

Bojar, R. M. (2011). *Manual of perioperative care in adult cardiac surgery* (5th ed.). West Sussex, UK: Wiley-Blackwell.

Gould, C. V., Umscheid, C. A., Agarwal, R. K., Kuntz, G., Pegues, D. A., & the Healthcare Infection Control Practices Advisory Committee (HICPAC). (2009). Guideline for prevention of catheter-associated urinary tract infections 2009. Retrieved from http://www.cdc.gov/hicpac/pdf/CAUTI/CAUTIguideline2009final.pdf.

Jacobson, C., Marzlin, K., & Webner, C. (2007). *Cardiovascular nursing practice*. Burien, WA: Cardiovascular Nursing Education Associates.

# 13

# Complications:
# Extended Recovery Period

*Complications of cardiac surgery may occur at many points along the path to recovery. This chapter is a continuation of Chapter 10 and deals with complications that tend to occur later in the hospital stay, often after patients are transferred out of the intensive care unit (ICU). However, complications discussed in Chapter 10 may occur late in the hospital stay and complications discussed in this chapter may occur early. Either way, it is important to be aware of potential complications and recognize them early so treatment can be started. In addition, stroke is a major complication of cardiac surgery and can be life changing and very distressing to the patient and family. Stroke may occur at any point in a patient's recovery and is discussed in Chapter 14.*

*Patients who have extended hospital stays may also experience other complications related to hospitalization. These complications are outside the scope of this book, but it is important to prevent these complications or, if that is not possible, to recognize and treat them if they do occur. These complications may include pressure ulcers; complications of prolonged ventilation, such as tracheotomy; loss of muscle mass and debilitation; failure to thrive; poor nutrition and need for tube feeding; and infections, including urinary tract infection and various infections with drug-resistant organisms.*

## Objectives

In this chapter, you will learn:

1. Prevention and treatment of common post-op cardiac surgery complications that may occur later in a patient's hospital stay
2. Assessment, laboratory, and x-ray findings that may signal potential complications

# CONDUCTION PROBLEMS

A number of arrhythmias and other conduction problems may arise after cardiac surgery. Arrhythmias may originate in the atria, the atrioventricular (AV) node, or the ventricles. Any arrhythmia has the potential to decrease cardiac output, which is detrimental to patients after heart surgery. It is imperative that nurses be able to recognize arrhythmias and know what actions to take.

## Atrial Fibrillation

Atrial fibrillation is a common complication of cardiac surgery and frequently prolongs hospital stay. (See Chapter 7 for a description of atrial fibrillation.) It occurs in 20% to 50% of cardiac surgery patients (Coventry, 2014). The incidence varies with the type of surgery, occurring more frequently after valve surgery or combination coronary artery bypass and valve surgery. This is because of the enlargement of the atria due to valve disease as well as incisions made in the atria while accessing a valve for either repair or replacement. This disruption of atrial tissue predisposes the patient to developing atrial fibrillation.

Atrial fibrillation typically develops 1 to 3 days after surgery. The risk increases with age, with elderly patients at highest risk of developing post-op atrial fibrillation. Other risk factors include preexisting atrial arrhythmias, previous cardiac surgery, low serum potassium or magnesium, valvular heart disease, and atrial enlargement. Manipulation of atrial tissue, fluid overload, electrolyte shifts, cooling, inflammatory response due to cardiopulmonary bypass, ischemia, and pericarditis increase the likelihood of atrial fibrillation.

Atrial fibrillation causes a decrease in cardiac output of up to 20% due to loss of atrial kick. Many patients do not tolerate such a decrease in cardiac output after cardiac surgery, so the goal is to restore normal sinus rhythm, rather than merely maintain a controlled rate. Patients who have been in atrial fibrillation for more than 6 months prior to surgery will most likely not be successfully converted into normal sinus rhythm, so the goal for these patients will be to control the ventricular response rate to less than 100 beats per minute.

## Prevention

There is evidence that the routine administration of magnesium sulfate prior to and immediately after cardiac surgery may decrease the rate of atrial fibrillation. Daily administration of metoprolol (Lopressor), 25–50 mg orally, has been shown to decrease the rate of atrial fibrillation after surgery. When giving metoprolol (Lopressor), blood pressure and heart rate should be monitored, since beta-blockers cause a decrease in both. Prophylactic oral amiodarone (Cordarone), 200–600 mg, may be given daily after cardiac surgery to patients at highest risk of developing post-op atrial fibrillation. Patients taking amiodarone (Cordarone) should be monitored for bradycardia, prolonged QT interval, and heart blocks.

## Assessment

After cardiac surgery, heart rhythm should be continuously monitored. Vital signs should be checked, especially blood pressure, heart rate, respiratory rate, and pulse oximetry. When in atrial fibrillation, the patient needs to be monitored for hemodynamic stability. Signs of hemodynamic instability include hypotension, changes in mental status, impaired peripheral perfusion, and decreased urine output. In addition, some patients become short of breath or lightheaded when in atrial fibrillation and some patients feel palpitations. Patients who have converted to atrial fibrillation should be assisted to bed or asked to remain in bed until their response can be determined.

## Diagnostics

A 12-lead electrocardiogram (ECG) should be performed for any patient who goes into atrial fibrillation. Serum electrolytes, especially potassium and magnesium, may be drawn as well so that these electrolytes may be quickly replaced if blood levels have fallen below parameters specified by the physician.

## Intervention

Patients in atrial fibrillation are treated either by restoring normal sinus rhythm or by controlling the ventricular response rate. The decision of how to treat is made based on the patient's history and hemodynamic stability while in atrial fibrillation. This decision should be made by the physician, who should be notified as soon as the patient goes into atrial fibrillation. Patients who are hemodynamically unstable need to be treated immediately. More time may be taken to try various treatment methods for patients who are hemodynamically stable and tolerating the rhythm.

Synchronized cardioversion is commonly used to convert a patient back into normal sinus rhythm. This involves the use of electrical current synchronized to the patient's QRS complex. A patient who is hemodynamically unstable in atrial fibrillation should have immediate synchronized cardioversion. Cardioversion is more successful if antiarrhythmic medications are given first. For patients who are not hemodynamically unstable in atrial fibrillation, an antiarrhythmic medication may be tried first, followed by synchronized cardioversion if the patient does not convert to normal sinus rhythm with medical therapy alone. Antiarrhythmic medications include amiodarone (Cordarone) and ibutilide (Corvert). Metoprolol (Lopressor) and diltiazem (Cardizem) may also be used.

For some patients, especially those with a history of permanent atrial fibrillation prior to surgery and those who are hemodynamically stable, the decision is made to control the rate of atrial fibrillation rather than try to convert to normal sinus rhythm. Also, if attempts to convert to normal sinus rhythm are unsuccessful, rate control may be the best option. Keeping the ventricular response rate less than 100 beats per minute increases ventricular filling time and thus increases cardiac output. If rate control is desired, beta-blockers, calcium channel blockers, and digoxin are most commonly used.

**CLINICAL ALERT!** Patients in atrial fibrillation for more than a few hours need anticoagulation due to stasis of blood in the atria and potential for forming clots, which then embolize to other areas of the body. Usually, a heparin infusion is administered until warfarin can be given to raise the international normalized ratio (INR) to between 2 and 3.

▶ **NURSING IMPLICATIONS:** The cardiac surgery nurse needs to be aware of the heart rhythm when caring for patients. New atrial fibrillation should be recognized and patient assessment for hemodynamic stability should take place immediately. The information gathered during the assessment should be relayed to the physician so a treatment plan may be decided. The nurse should anticipate immediate synchronized cardioversion for unstable patients.

*ESSENTIAL FACTS*

Atrial fibrillation is very common after cardiac surgery and can cause a decrease in cardiac output and hemodynamic instability. When a patient is in atrial fibrillation, action should be taken to convert the patient to normal sinus rhythm or control the ventricular response rate.

## Conduction Blocks

During cardiac surgery, the AV node may be damaged either by surgical manipulation or by edema. This may lead to the development of various types of heart block (type I, type II—Wenckebach or Mobitz II, or complete heart block). These blocks may be transient, especially if caused by edema, but may cause a dangerously low heart rate and decrease in cardiac output.

### Prevention

All patients should have heart rate and rhythm monitored after cardiac surgery. The physician should be notified of any heart block so that appropriate treatment may be initiated.

### Assessment

As described earlier for atrial fibrillation, patients who develop a conduction block should be assessed for hemodynamic stability. Vital signs should be taken, mental status and alertness should be assessed, and patients' subjective feeling of well-being should be determined. It is important to discern whether or not tissues are being perfused.

### Diagnostics

A 12-lead ECG should be performed to determine the exact nature of the conduction block.

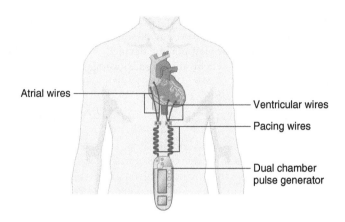

Atrial wires

Ventricular wires

Pacing wires

Dual chamber pulse generator

**FIGURE 13.1** Pacing using epicardial pacing wires.

## Intervention

Patients who develop a conduction block and experience hemodynamic instability should be paced, as ordered by a physician. If epicardial pacing wires are in place, these wires should be attached to a pacemaker generator and pacing should begin at a rate sufficient to perfuse the tissues and maintain cardiac output (Figure 13.1). If there are no epicardial pacing wires and the patient has a low blood pressure or other signs of severe hemodynamic instability, transcutaneous pacing should be initiated. Transcutaneous pacing is painful. Pain medication should be administered per physician's order and placement of a transvenous pacing wire should take place as soon as possible. For patients who are less emergent, a transvenous pacing wire may be placed and transvenous pacing initiated without first pacing transcutaneously.

If a patient requires pacing and the conduction block does not resolve within a day or two, a permanent pacemaker may be required. If needed, a permanent pacemaker will be placed prior to discharge.

▶ **NURSING IMPLICATIONS:** Assessment of patient stability should occur immediately if a patient develops a conduction block. The physician should be notified immediately if a patient becomes bradycardic or hemodynamically unstable with a conduction block. The cardiac surgery nurse should anticipate when pacing may be ordered and gather necessary supplies.

Conduction blocks affecting the AV node occur frequently after cardiac surgery and may be transient or permanent. A low heart rate with hemodynamic instability requires pacing.

## Ventricular Arrhythmias

Premature ventricular complexes (PVCs), ventricular tachycardia (VT), or ventricular fibrillation (VF) may occur after cardiac surgery, but are less common than atrial dysrhythmias. PVCs are common and not usually worrisome as long as serum potassium and magnesium are maintained at normal levels. Transient VT is also common and may be related to reperfusion injury. Ventricular arrhythmias are more common in patients with recent myocardial infarction (MI) or perioperative MI, poor left ventricular function, prolonged cardiopulmonary bypass time, and need for inotropes or an intraaortic balloon pump post-op.

### Prevention

Maintaining serum potassium above 4 mg/dL and serum magnesium above 2 mg/dL will prevent some ventricular arrhythmias. Some surgeons prefer to keep serum potassium higher (4.5 or 5 mg/dL) to prevent arrhythmias.

### Assessment

Patients who develop ventricular arrhythmias should be immediately assessed for hemodynamic stability.

**CLINICAL ALERT!** Patients who experience hemodynamically unstable ventricular arrhythmias require immediate intervention using advanced cardiac life support (ACLS) protocols to prevent death.

### Diagnostics

Patients who develop PVCs or VT and who are stable may benefit from a 12-lead ECG to determine the exact nature of the arrhythmia. Use of the atrial epicardial lead to determine atrial versus

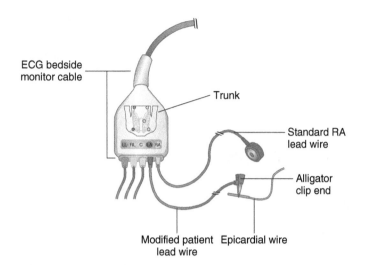

**FIGURE 13.2** One of the atrial epicardial pacing wires can be used to obtain an atrial electrogram. This aids in differentiating tachycardias of supraventricular from those of ventricular origin.

ventricular origin of any tachyarrhythmia is recommended, as outlined here (Drew et al., 2004):

- The atrial electrogram can be recorded with the bedside monitor or with a standard 12-lead ECG machine (Figure 13.2). The simplest way to record an immediate atrial electrogram at the bedside is to unsnap the chest (V) lead wire from the patient's chest and hold it against the tip of an atrial epicardial pacemaker lead wire so that metal is touching metal.
- Rubber gloves should be worn when handling epicardial pacemaker leads because a small amount of current traveling up the wire directly to the heart can induce VF in a vulnerable patient (Drew et al., 2004).
- The atrial electrogram magnifies atrial activity in a rhythm strip, showing even P waves that are buried in a QRS complex. For example, in a patient with a preexisting bundle branch block, it can be difficult to tell if a tachycardia is atrial fibrillation with rapid ventricular response or VT, but an atrial electrogram can show if there is atrial activity.

Serum potassium and magnesium should also be drawn. Patients who are hemodynamically unstable require immediate intervention and treatment should not be delayed to obtain a 12-lead ECG.

Serum electrolytes should still be drawn while other interventions are taking place.

### Intervention

PVCs or VT occurring in patients who are hemodynamically stable may be treated by finding and fixing the underlying cause. This may include searching for evidence of ischemia or replacing serum potassium and magnesium. Inotropes should be avoided in patients with ventricular arrhythmias. For VT, an antiarrhythmic medication such as amiodarone (Cordarone) or lidocaine may be ordered to convert the rhythm to normal sinus rhythm. For patients who develop hemodynamically unstable VT or VF, immediate action must be taken following ACLS protocols.

▶ **NURSING IMPLICATIONS:** Serum magnesium and potassium should be kept within ordered parameters. Nurses should be alert to potentially life-threatening rhythm changes and take immediate action.

### ESSENTIAL FACTS

Ventricular arrhythmias are less common than atrial arrhythmias but are more life-threatening. The bedside nurse should be ready to follow ACLS protocols to restore a normal rhythm.

## NEUROLOGICAL DYSFUNCTION

Neurological complications after cardiac surgery can be very severe, affecting mortality and quality of life. Up to 50% of patients may experience some cognitive impairment during the first week following cardiac surgery and many still have cognitive impairment 6 weeks after surgery. Neurological complications increase the likelihood a patient will be discharged to a rehabilitation facility or long-term care facility instead of to home. Risk factors include advanced age (older than 70 years), history of pulmonary disease or hypertension, diabetes, history of unstable angina or neuro deficits, history of excessive alcohol consumption, post-op dysrhythmias, and prior cardiac surgery. Aortic atherosclerosis and carotid artery disease are also risk factors because pieces of plaque can break free during surgery and embolize into cerebral arteries. Carotid artery disease, which limits blood flow, may also contribute to cerebral ischemia during low flow states.

Neurological complications following cardiac surgery fall into two categories. The first category (type I) includes stroke, transient ischemic attack (TIA), focal deficits, and coma. The second category (type II) includes confusion, agitation, decline in intellectual functioning, disorientation, and memory deficits. Type I complications come with significant mortality and greatly increase hospital stay. Type II complications are more common and have a lower mortality rate; they also may increase hospital length of stay. Collectively, type II complications are often referred to as encephalopathy. Stroke is covered in Chapter 14.

Mild cognitive decline is common after surgery and may include memory deficits and difficulty with problem solving, attention, and ability to learn. Most patients report improvement within 1 to 2 months after surgery.

## Prevention

For high-risk patients, there are preventative strategies that may be employed in the operating room. For example, avoiding aortic manipulation in patients with aortic atherosclerosis can decrease risk. Nurses also play a large role in prevention of neurological complications by avoiding hyperthermia during rewarming, post-op hypotension, and hyperglycemia, all of which may increase the risk of these complications.

## Assessment

Neuro assessments should be performed routinely on all cardiac surgery patients. Stroke should be suspected if the patient fails to awaken, follow commands, or move extremities when sedation is discontinued after surgery. Focal deficits should also be noted: facial droop, weakness on one side, aphasia, visual changes, or pupil changes. Unfortunately, assessment is often difficult due to emergence from anesthesia and response to various medications. Patients suspected of having a stroke should be seen by a neurologist and undergo brain imaging to confirm the diagnosis. (See Chapter 14 for more information.)

Post-op encephalopathy is more difficult to diagnose and to manage. These patients may experience delirium, demonstrated by inattention, cognitive impairment, memory deficits, disorientation, perceptual changes, and inappropriate speech. These acute changes may also be accompanied by agitation. Agitation is extreme vocal or motor behavior that is unsafe for the patient or for hospital staff. Delirium and agitation often occur together, but delirium may occur without agitation. Use of a validated tool, such as the Confusion Assessment Method for the ICU (CAM-ICU), to determine if the patient is experiencing delirium will assist in diagnosing and treating this condition.

## Diagnostics

Patients suspected of having delirium should have electrolytes as well as renal and liver function tests and an arterial blood gas drawn to help determine the cause of the delirium. Causes of delirium are discussed in Table 13.1.

## Intervention

Treatment of encephalopathy and delirium includes searching for and treating the underlying cause, providing a supportive

---

**TABLE 13.1 THINK Acronym to Remember the Potential Causes of Delirium**

Toxic situations

- Congestive heart failure, shock, dehydration
- Deliriogenic medications (tight titration of sedatives)
- New organ failure (e.g., liver, kidney)

Hypoxemia
Infection/sepsis (nosocomial)
Immobilization
Nonpharmacological interventions (Are these being neglected?)

- Hearing aids, glasses, sleep protocols, music, noise control, ambulation

K+ or electrolyte problems

*Source:* Balas et al. (2012).

environment, and using medications and nonpharmacological interventions to treat symptoms of delirium. Causes of delirium are outlined in Table 13.1. Pain medications and many cardiac medications may lead to delirium, especially in elderly patients. Medications, especially those newly administered, should be reviewed carefully to determine if any may be causing delirium. If an underlying cause for post-op encephalopathy or delirium cannot be found, it may be a consequence of surgery. Often, encephalopathy and delirium improve once a patient is transferred out of the ICU. While delirium is present, a supportive environment should be provided. Patients should be reassured and reoriented frequently. Patient safety should be maintained during this time. An excellent resource for management of delirium is a website sponsored by the Delirium and Cognitive Impairment Study Group at Vanderbilt University: www.icudelirium.org.

▶ **NURSING IMPLICATIONS:** Careful neuro assessments, noting any changes from baseline, are important for early identification of neurological problems. For the elderly and other high-risk patients, both patients and family members should be made aware prior to surgery about the potential for cognitive deficits, confusion, and agitation after surgery. For patients who do experience these complications, a protective and supportive environment should be provided. Family members may also require emotional support, especially if their loved one is agitated.

## ESSENTIAL FACTS

Neurological complications following cardiac surgery are a major cause of mortality and morbidity. Patients should be monitored for focal deficits as well as delirium and cognitive impairment. A search should be made for potentially reversible causes of these symptoms.

## INFECTION

Wound infections can be serious and life-threatening. Nurses caring for cardiac surgery patients play a large role in prevention of infection as well as early recognition. Infection may occur in any surgical wound: midline sternotomy, chest incisions for minimally invasive or port surgeries, graft donor sites on the arms or legs, or

**TABLE 13.2 Risk Factors for Wound Infections Following Cardiac Surgery**

| Pre-Op Risk | Intra-Op Risk | Post-Op Risk |
| --- | --- | --- |
| Diabetes | Use of both internal mammary arteries | Chest left open beyond surgical period |
| Advanced age | Prolonged operating time (greater than 4 hours) | Need to reopen the chest |
| Obesity | | |
| Large breast size | | |
| Lung disease | Long cardiopulmonary bypass time | Transfusion of more than 5 units of blood |
| Pre-op hospital stay of greater than 5 days | | Prolonged mechanical ventilation |
| Poor nutrition | Prolonged hypothermia (beyond surgical period) | Prolonged cardiopulmonary resuscitation (CPR) |
| Renal failure | | |
| Respiratory disease | | |
| Smoking | | Low cardiac output |
| Immunosuppression | | Sternal instability |
| Steroid use | | Infection elsewhere in the body |

chest tube insertion sites. Risk factors for wound infections are listed in Table 13.2.

Surgical site infections (SSIs) are classified according to severity and depth based on underlying structures affected. A superficial SSI involves the skin and subcutaneous tissues at the incision site. A deep SSI involves muscle, fascia, or bone (usually the sternum below a midline sternotomy incision) underneath the surgical incision. An organ or space SSI involves the heart itself or tissues in the mediastinum (tissues underneath the sternum). These classifications are used for infections that occur within the first 30 days or, if an implant was left in place, for the first year after the surgery. Most cardiac surgeries involve leaving an implant (valve replacement or valve ring, sternal wires, clips or other markers).

## Prevention

Several steps may be taken prior to surgery to prevent infection. These steps should be followed whenever possible but may not be possible for patients undergoing emergency surgery. Consequently, they will have higher risk of infection.

Patients with preexisting infections should have these treated prior to surgery. This will reduce the risk of cross-contamination. Hair should be removed from the surgical site by careful clipping. Care should be taken to prevent nicking the skin, which increases risk of infection. This is why hair is clipped rather than shaved. Cleansing of the skin with antibacterial soap is important to decrease the bacterial count prior to surgery. This should be done, at a minimum, the night before surgery and should include all body areas where incisions may be made. In the operating room, the incision site should be cleansed with chlorhexidine gluconate or povidone–iodine before the incision is made. In addition to all of these measures, prophylactic antibiotics should be administered prior to surgery and for up to 48 hours after surgery.

After surgery, meticulous handwashing is one of the most important ways to prevent surgical infections. Glucose control is also critical to reduce infection risk. After cardiac surgery, blood glucose should not be allowed to rise above 180 mg/dL. This is true for diabetic patients as well as patients who are not previously known to be diabetic.

Incisions should be protected from infectious materials. A sterile dressing should be maintained over incisions initially. Although the time frame for leaving sterile dressings in place varies by institution, it is usually between 24 and 72 hours. After this time, dressings may be removed and the incision left open to air unless there is drainage from the wound. Once incisions are open to air, care should be taken to prevent contaminated equipment from touching incisions. Equipment such as ECG leads, blood pressure cuffs, and stethoscopes should be cleaned meticulously or disposable equipment should be used.

## Assessment

Once sterile dressings have been removed, incisions should be assessed at least once a shift. Signs of infection in an incision include incision edges that are not approximated, excessive pain or tenderness, redness, odor, swelling, and drainage—especially if drainage is thick, purulent or green, or has an odor. If a patient has a sudden increase in incisional pain, this is an indication of infection. Drainage of serosanguinous fluid from leg incisions is common and is not necessarily indicative of infection unless accompanied by other signs of infection. Drainage of any fluid from a sternal incision is often the first sign of a developing sternal wound infection.

Radial and sternal incisions require additional assessments. If popping or clicking is heard in the sternal incision, or if the patient states that he or she hears popping or clicking, the surgeon should be notified. This indicates an unstable sternum and may be a sign of infection. Patients who have radial incisions should have an assessment made of circulation in the affected hand. Assessment should include color, temperature, capillary refill time, and ulnar pulse.

Patients should also be assessed for systemic infection. Fever, chills, and an elevated white blood cell (WBC) count may indicate infection in a surgical incision.

## Diagnostics

To definitively diagnose a wound infection and determine what organism is responsible, a wound culture should be obtained. An x-ray, computed tomography (CT) scan, or magnetic resonance imaging (MRI) scan may be helpful to determine the depth of infection prior to sternal debridement.

## Intervention

Treatment depends on the extent of the infection. A superficial SSI may be treated with antibiotics alone. Often, intravenous antibiotics are initially ordered by the physician and the patient is sent home on oral antibiotics. Deep SSIs often require surgical debridement in addition to antibiotics. Negative pressure wound therapy is often ordered to speed healing of the wound.

Treatment of a deep SSI involving a sternal wound will involve debridement and may involve placement of catheters to continuously infuse an antibiotic solution. If there is involvement of the bone, the infected portion of the sternum will need to be removed. If it is necessary to remove the entire sternum, a muscle flap may be placed over the heart, using the pectoralis major or the rectus muscles. Placement of a muscle flap is usually performed by a plastic surgeon.

▶ **NURSING IMPLICATIONS:** The cardiac surgery nurse is pivotal to infection prevention practices. If signs of infection are noted prior to surgery, the surgeon should be notified. This may include an elevated WBC count, bacteria noted in a urinalysis, or a skin infection such as a yeast infection or cellulitis. Strict hand-washing will prevent many infections. Proper incision care and cleaning of equipment that will touch the patient are also critical to prevent infection.

Many infections do not become evident until after patient discharge. Patient education about the signs and symptoms of infection is important to early identification of infection. Patients and families should know what their incisions look like upon discharge so they will know if there is a change. They should also know who to call if infection is suspected.

## *ESSENTIAL FACTS*

Infection is a very serious complication of cardiac surgery and may be life-threatening. Early identification is critical, since early treatment improves outcomes.

## HEPARIN-INDUCED THROMBOCYTOPENIA

Thrombocytopenia is a decrease in platelet count. There are many causes of thrombocytopenia that occur with cardiac surgery, such as destruction of platelets during cardiopulmonary bypass and hemodilution. One significant cause of thrombocytopenia is a response to heparin. Heparin-induced thrombocytopenia (HIT) is caused when platelet-activating antibodies form in response to heparin. This platelet activation leads to thrombin formation and a hypercoagulable state. Cardiac surgery patients are at risk due to previous exposure to heparin during cardiac catheterization, large doses, and long exposure to heparin during surgery. HIT can have very unfortunate thrombotic consequences for patients. Various body parts and organs, including extremities, may lose blood supply and become necrotic due to thrombosis.

### Prevention

Heparin exposure should be avoided whenever possible. Most institutions have policies in place to reduce heparin exposure, such as using saline instead of heparin to lock peripheral and central lines and in arterial line flush solutions. Nurses play an important role in recognizing signs of HIT early so treatment may be instituted. Early treatment may prevent consequences of HIT due to excessive clotting.

## Assessment

Patients should be assessed for clinical signs and symptoms of thrombosis. Skin temperature and color should be assessed. Any skin lesions or abnormal sensations should be noted. Peripheral pulses should be monitored carefully. Monitoring should occur for signs and symptoms of stroke, MI, pulmonary embolism, or renal impairment, all of which may occur as the result of thrombosis.

## Diagnostics

A diagnosis of HIT should be considered if the platelet count falls to less than 150,000 mm3 or by greater than 50% of baseline measurement. This fall in platelet count typically occurs between 5 and 14 days after the first heparin exposure. Cardiac surgery patients often receive heparin during an angiogram prior to surgery, so alterations in platelet count may appear sooner than 5 days after surgery. A confirmatory antibody test should also be sent to the laboratory.

## Intervention

**CLINICAL ALERT!** When HIT is suspected, all heparin-containing products must be discontinued. This includes heparin in any flush solutions as well as heparin-coated catheters. Because HIT is a thrombotic disorder, a nonheparin anticoagulant should be administered, even before HIT is confirmed by laboratory data. Argatroban (Acova), lepirudin (Refludan), and bivalirudin (Angiomax) are all non–heparin-containing direct thrombin inhibitors that may be administered to prevent thrombosis from HIT.

▶ **NURSING IMPLICATIONS:** The cardiac surgery nurse should watch for a drop in platelet count and notify the physician if a significant drop occurs. Early identification and treatment is important to prevent thrombosis. If HIT is suspected, treatment should begin before confirmatory lab test results are obtained. If clinical signs of HIT are present, the physician may continue treatment with anticoagulants even if a lab result is negative.

## ESSENTIAL FACTS

HIT is a serious complication of heparin administration. Despite a drop in platelet count, it is a prothrombotic condition and often causes thromboses which may lead to organ dysfunction or loss of limbs.

## RENAL FAILURE

Post-op acute kidney injury may occur in 2% to 3% of cardiac surgery patients, depending on the definition used (e.g., increase in serum creatinine or decrease in glomerular filtration rate of a certain amount). Only about 1% of these patients require dialysis or other renal replacement therapy. Many risk factors are implicated in post-op acute kidney injury, including pre-op renal dysfunction, peripheral arterial disease, advanced age, race, female sex, diabetes requiring insulin, emergency surgery, pre-op intraaortic balloon pump, and congestive heart failure or shock (Hillis et al., 2011). The major cause of renal insufficiency and failure is poor perfusion to the kidneys.

### Prevention

Nurses play an important role in prevention of renal failure. Maintaining renal perfusion by optimizing preload and cardiac output are the primary post-op concerns in preventing renal failure. For patients with renal insufficiency, becoming knowledgeable about nephrotoxic medications and avoiding administration of them postoperatively is important to prevent progression of renal disease.

### Assessment

Urine output should be monitored closely in the post-op period. If urine output falls to less than 0.5 mL/kg/hr, the physician should be notified so steps can be taken to prevent renal insufficiency and failure.

## Diagnostics

A complete metabolic panel should be drawn per physician's order immediately upon arrival from the operating room and periodically thereafter. A serum creatinine level of greater than 2 mg/dL or a steadily climbing serum creatinine signifies renal insufficiency.

## Intervention

Hypotension, decreased preload, and decreased cardiac output should be avoided in patients at risk for or experiencing renal insufficiency. If serum creatinine continues to rise, a nephrologist may be consulted. Hemodialysis or other renal replacement therapies may be attempted in hopes that renal function will return. If renal function does not improve, lifelong dialysis may be necessary.

**CLINICAL ALERT!** Use of diuretics and renal dose dopamine in patients with renal insufficiency is controversial. Diuretics often increase urine output but may decrease preload and thus blood flow to the kidneys, exacerbating the problem. Renal dose dopamine is still used by some surgeons in an attempt to increase blood flow to the kidneys. However, although low-dose dopamine increases urine output and decreases serum creatinine, there is no evidence that its use improves survival or decreases the incidence of renal failure (Hillis et al., 2011).

▶ **NURSING IMPLICATIONS:** Cardiac surgery nurses play a large role in prevention of renal insufficiency and failure by managing hemodynamics. Hypotension and decreased cardiac output are major culprits and should be avoided. Nurses should work with pharmacists to identify nephrotoxic medications that should be avoided. For example, ibuprofin (Advil, Motrin) and ketorolac (Toradol) are nephrotoxic; also, many antibiotics are nephrotoxic or require dosage adjustments in patients with renal insufficiency.

## ESSENTIAL FACTS

Many factors during the perioperative period may predispose a patient to renal complications. Nurses have a very important role in maintaining blood pressure and cardiac output to prevent continuing damage to the kidneys that may lead to renal failure.

## GASTROINTESTINAL COMPLICATIONS

Gastrointestinal (GI) complications occur in only about 0.1% to 1% of cardiac surgery patients (Hillis et al., 2011). For those who do experience GI complications, mortality is about 50%. Most GI complications do not become symptomatic until post-op day 6 or 7. Risk factors include prolonged cardiopulmonary bypass time, prolonged mechanical ventilation, septic shock, and renal complications.

Perioperative hypotension and low cardiac output may cause ischemia in the mesenteric and splanchnic arterial beds resulting in intestinal ischemia. Other GI complications include ileus, upper GI bleed, acute pancreatitis, cholecystitis, and acute hepatic failure.

### Prevention

Maintaining an adequate blood pressure and cardiac output will prevent some of these complications.

### Assessment

Symptoms may be vague and are often atypical. Patients often have a hard time describing symptoms that occur as a result of GI complications, making them extremely hard to diagnose.

### Diagnostics

Laboratory data, including a complete blood count and complete metabolic panel, may be helpful in diagnosing a GI complication.

If GI complications are suspected, an abdominal x-ray may be helpful. An endoscopy will be used to diagnose a GI bleed.

## Intervention

GI complications should be treated symptomatically and patients should be given supportive treatment. A GI specialist may be consulted for specialized treatment. Patients experiencing a GI bleed may have the area of bleeding located and cauterized using endoscopy.

▶ **NURSING IMPLICATIONS:** Nurses can prevent some GI complications by preventing hypotension and low cardiac output.

## ESSENTIAL FACTS

GI complications are rare but have a very high mortality rate. They are often difficult to diagnose and may occur late in the patient's hospital stay or after discharge.

## POSTPERICARDIOTOMY SYNDROME

Postpericardiotomy syndrome is an autoimmune response causing inflammation of the pericardium. This syndrome may appear weeks to months after surgery. Pericardial effusion is usually present and may be so severe that cardiac tamponade develops. Postpericardiotomy syndrome may also contribute to early graft closure and restrictive pericarditis.

## Prevention

Since this syndrome usually appears after discharge, the best prevention is to make patients aware of what symptoms to watch for and when to call the physician. However, there is some evidence that prophylactic administration of nonsteroidal anti-inflammatory medications (NSAIDs) or colchicine (Colcrys) may prevent some cases of postpericardiotomy syndrome.

## Assessment

Patients should be assessed for precordial chest pain and a pericardial rub. Fever, malaise, and possibly joint pain may also be present.

## Diagnostics

WBC count and eosinophils will be elevated. Erythrocyte sedimentation rate, which is a marker of inflammation, also will be elevated. A chest x-ray typically shows pericardial effusion. Echocardiography may be used to detect pericardial effusion or cardiac tamponade.

### Intervention

Initial treatment of patients with postpericardiotomy syndrome includes diuretics and aspirin. If this is not effective, a course of NSAIDs is usually effective. If symptoms continue, steroids may be used. If a pericardial effusion is large or causes symptoms, pericardiocentesis may be performed to drain the fluid.

▶ **NURSING IMPLICATIONS:** Upon discharge, patients should know what symptoms to watch for and who to call if those symptoms appear. If patients are sent home with prophylactic medications for postpericardiotomy syndrome, they should understand the rationale.

## *ESSENTIAL FACTS*

Postpericardiotomy syndrome is an inflammatory condition that may occur weeks to months after cardiac surgery.

## DEPRESSION

Many patients with cardiovascular disease have depressive symptoms, and patients with depression have higher rates of morbidity and mortality. Patients who show depressive symptoms before or after cardiac surgery have higher complication rates. The link between depression and complications after cardiac surgery is not fully understood, but depression appears to cause real physiological changes, such as increased platelet reactivity and decreased heart rate variability (which has been linked with increased sudden death after MI). In addition, depressed patients are less likely to adhere to a prescribed medication regimen and make the lifestyle changes necessary to decrease cardiovascular risk factors.

Symptoms of depression appear to peak several days after surgery and diminish over time. Pain, sleep deprivation, and loss of control may contribute to these feelings.

## Prevention

While preventing depression after cardiac surgery may not be possible, recognition and treatment is important to reduce the risks associated with depression.

## Assessment

Depression can be very difficult to assess after cardiac surgery. Patients who seem uninterested in activities (talking with family members, eating, self-care, ambulating) or who express feelings of depression or hopelessness may require further intervention.

## Diagnostics

No diagnostic or laboratory tests reveal depression. However, several validated questionnaires that may be administered by a social worker or trained mental health practitioner may demonstrate the presence and severity of depression.

## Intervention

Patients who are known to be depressed and were on antidepressants prior to surgery should be restarted on these as soon as possible after surgery. Patients who are experiencing less severe depressive symptoms may be helped by encouraging them to connect with family and friends or perform activities that provide a sense of accomplishment.

Negative perceptions, beliefs or thoughts may play a role in depression after cardiac surgery. Patients may feel they will never again be able to work or do the things they enjoy. Education about recovery from cardiac surgery may help patients with these feelings.

Patients with severe depressive symptoms or who are not helped by connecting with family and friends or by learning about recovery from surgery need additional intervention. A social worker or mental health professional should be consulted while the patient is in the hospital. Resources should be provided upon discharge to help depressed patients. Cardiac rehabilitation programs include assistance with depression and other psychosocial problems.

▶ **NURSING IMPLICATIONS:** Nurses are in a unique position to notice patient behavior that may indicate depression. While depression is common after surgery, it should be treated to reduce the increased complications that are associated with it. Patients and family members should be made aware that depression may occur and given guidance about who to contact for help if needed.

## *ESSENTIAL FACTS*

Depression is a common and serious occurrence after cardiac surgery. It is associated with a higher morbidity and mortality than is seen in nondepressed patients. Early recognition is key in beginning treatment.

## REFERENCES

Balas, M. C., Vasilevskis, E. E., Burke, W. J., Boehm, L., Pun, B.T., Olsen, K. M., . . . Ely, E. W. (2012). Critical care nurses' role in implementing the "ABCDE bundle" into practice. *Critical Care Nurse, 32*(2), 35-48

Coventry, B. J. (Ed.). (2014). *Cardio-thoracic, vascular, renal and transplant surgery*. London, UK: Springer.

Drew, B. J., Califf, R. M., Funk, M., Kaufman, E. S., Krucoff, M. W., Laks, M. M., . . . American Heart Association. (2004). Practice standards for electrocardiographic monitoring in hospital settings: An American Heart Association scientific statement from the councils on cardiovascular nursing, clinical cardiology, and cardiovascular disease in the young. *Circulation, 110*, 2721–2746.

Hillis, L. D. , Smith, P. K., Anderson, J. L., Bittl, J. A., Bridges, C. R., Byrne, J. G., . . . Winniford, M. D. (2011). 2011 ACCF/AHA guideline for coronary artery bypass graft surgery: A report of the American College of Cardiology Foundation/American Heart Association Task Force on Practice Guidelines. *Journal of the American College of Cardiology, 58,* e123–210.

## BIBLIOGRAPHY

Bell, L. & Sargood, T. (2007). Atrial electrograms after cardiac surgery. *American Journal of Critical Care, 16,* 360.

Bojar, R. M. (2011). *Manual of perioperative care in adult cardiac surgery* (5th ed.). West Sussex, UK: Wiley-Blackwell.

Hardin, S. R., & Kaplow, R. (Eds.). (2010). *Cardiac surgery essentials for critical care nursing.* Sudbury, MA: Jones & Bartlett.

Jacobson, C., Marzlin, K., & Webner, C. (2007). *Cardiovascular nursing practice.* Burien, WA: Cardiovascular Nursing Education Associates.

McRae, M. E., Chan, A., & Imperial-Perez, F. (2010). Cardiac surgical nurses' use of atrial electrograms to improve diagnosis of arrhythmia. *American Journal of Critical Care, 19,* 124–134.

# 14

## Stroke

*Patients undergoing cardiac surgery are at higher risk for stroke than the general population. Stroke increases morbidity and mortality of patients before and after surgery. In addition, diagnostic and treatment options for stroke may be limited due to recent surgery, anticoagulants, and presence of pacemaker wires or other devices. Cardiac diseases and neurological diseases are treated very differently, and the medical and nursing care of these patients is typically overseen by different specialists with very different skill sets. Cardiac surgery patients who experience a stroke may stay in a cardiac specialty unit for care, so it is critical that the nurses in these units know how to care for patients experiencing acute neurological issues.*

In this chapter, you will learn:

1. Signs and symptoms of stroke after cardiac surgery
2. Types of stroke, including treatment strategies for each type
3. Strategies to reduce secondary injury after a stroke has occurred

## RISK FACTORS FOR STROKE

Each year, approximately 795,000 people experience a new or recurrent stroke (ischemic or hemorrhagic). Approximately 610,000 of these are first attacks and 185,000 are recurrent attacks. On average, every 40 seconds, someone in the United States has a stroke; every 4 minutes someone dies of one (Go et al., 2013).

The risk factors for stroke are nearly identical to those for cardiovascular disease. Patients with atherosclerotic disease of the coronary arteries frequently also have atherosclerotic disease of the cerebral, carotid, and peripheral arteries. This places patients with coronary artery disease at high risk for stroke before and after surgery.

The risk of stroke following coronary artery bypass surgery is 2% to 5% but is higher (5%–15%) following more complex surgeries, such as valve surgeries, ventricular aneurysm repair, or aortic arch surgeries. Risk factors for perioperative stroke include advanced age, aortic arch atherosclerotic disease, prior stroke or documented cerebrovascular disease, recent myocardial infarction, left ventricular dysfunction, hypertension, diabetes, chronic renal insufficiency, and atrial fibrillation. Longer cross-clamp times, longer time spent on cardiopulmonary bypass, and low cardiac output after surgery also increase the risk (Sila, 2012).

Carotid stenosis increases the risk of perioperative stroke. Patients at high risk for carotid artery disease (i.e., having one or more of the following: older than 65 years, left main coronary artery disease, peripheral arterial disease, history of transient ischemic attack [TIA] or stroke, hypertension, smoking, diabetes) may undergo a carotid artery duplex scan prior to surgery. Patients with a previous TIA or stroke with a significant (50%–99%) carotid artery stenosis may receive carotid revascularization in conjunction with cardiac surgery. This may consist of carotid artery stenting or an open carotid endarterectomy procedure. Carotid artery revascularization may be scheduled prior to or at the time of cardiac surgery, depending on patient needs and magnitude of carotid and cardiovascular disease (Hillis et al., 2011).

Despite the increased risk for stroke and other neurological complications experienced by patients with known cardiac disease, it is often difficult for nurses working with this patient population to recognize and manage acute stroke as this is not their area of expertise. However, the nursing care these patients receive is critical to their long-term outcomes. A few tips should be kept in mind to improve the care and outcomes for cardiac patients with neurological complications:

- Assess for and suspect stroke or other neurological dysfunction unless proven otherwise

- Know what diagnostic tests to expect and what information they provide
- Know the cause and extent of the stroke
- Watch for deterioration or extension of injury
- Prevent secondary injury

## NEUROLOGICAL ASSESSMENT

Neuro assessments should be performed routinely on all cardiac surgery patients. The basic neuro assessment should include the items listed in Table 14.1. The key is to look for changes from baseline. The baseline assessment is the presurgery assessment. If the patient experiences a stroke after surgery and has new neurological deficits, ongoing neuro assessments would be compared to the new, post-stroke baseline.

### TABLE 14.1  Basic Neuro Assessment

| Assessment Area | Key Considerations |
| --- | --- |
| Level of consciousness | Glasgow Coma Scale reveals arousal state (eye opening), content of consciousness (best verbal response), and both arousal and content of consciousness (best motor response). |
| Reaction of pupils | Check pupil size and reaction to light. The cranial nerves that control pupils are adjacent to the brain stem. Thus, papillary changes indicate the presence and level of brain stem dysfunction. Keep in mind that some drugs can affect pupils (e.g., atropine can cause fixed, dilated pupils and opiates can cause pinpoint pupils), but the effect will be seen symmetrically in both eyes. However, changes in pupil symmetry are a sign of late neurological decline. |
| Presence or absence of confusion | Confusion is a nonspecific sign that may signal serious dysfunction in the brain. |
| Speech pattern (slurred speech, aphasia) | This may signal ischemia or other damage to areas of the brain that control speech. |

(continued)

## TABLE 14.1 Basic Neuro Assessment (*continued*)

| | |
|---|---|
| Cranial nerve quick check | Look for equal movement of the face, eyes and mouth. <br> • Is the smile equal? <br> • If the patient sticks the tongue out, does it veer to one side? <br> • Is there feeling on both sides of the face? <br> • Does the patient have coordinated eye movements? <br> Can the patient shrug the shoulders? |
| Symmetrical strength and movement of arms and legs | Purposeful movement indicates proper functioning of the brain. Also look for equality of strength and movement. <br> Have the patient hold hands straight out and look for drift (much more sensitive to changes than grip strength). <br> Check for equality of strength in leg muscles. |
| Also pay attention to: | • Any changes in vision or visual field (e.g., patient does not notice items on one side of the room). If you suspect changes in vision, hold up two fingers to the patient's right side and ask, "How many fingers am I holding up?" Repeat on the left side. <br> • Loss of equilibrium, discoordination, balance. Can be indicative of posterior circulation strokes. <br> • Reports of unusual behavior by the patient's family. |

Stroke should be suspected if the patient fails to awaken, follow commands, or move extremities when sedation is discontinued after surgery. Unfortunately, assessment is often difficult due to emergence from anesthesia and response to various medications. However, it is important to remember that a delay from awakening from anesthesia is often the first clue to a perioperative neurological complication (Sila, 2012). Focal deficits should also be noted: facial droop, weakness on one side, aphasia, visual changes, or pupil changes.

While performing a neuro assessment, the nurse should keep in mind that several clinical situations mimic stroke symptoms. Hypoglycemia may produce symptoms identical to stroke and can be quickly treated or ruled out after obtaining a glucose measurement. A seizure may occur with stroke-like symptoms. A patient with a history of seizures should be maintained on seizure medications during hospitalization. A patient with complicated migraines may have stroke-like symptoms. Also, patients with a history of intravenous drug use or endocarditis, especially with a fever, may experience stroke symptoms in the presence of a brain abscess. However, patients with stroke symptoms after cardiac surgery should be assumed to be having a stroke unless there is definite evidence to the contrary.

When changes in the neuro assessment are discovered, it is important to determine *when* the changes occurred or when the patient was last seen normal (i.e., without the stroke symptoms). This is critical for determining treatment options. If the patient is slow to awaken from anesthesia or wakes up from anesthesia with focal neurological deficits, it is likely that the last seen normal time is at or before induction of anesthesia. If changes occur after awakening from anesthesia, the last seen normal time would be the last time a health care provider or possibly family member saw the patient without the stroke symptoms. Revascularization strategies are only helpful for a certain amount of time after symptoms occur, so the time at which the patient was last seen normal is critical. Patients suspected of having a stroke should be scheduled for a consultation with a neurologist, as available and per hospital protocol, and undergo brain imaging to confirm the diagnosis.

## ESSENTIAL FACTS

When it is suspected that a patient may be having a stroke, the most important information to gather is the onset time and the type and extent of symptoms. This will help determine what treatment options are available to the patient.

## DIAGNOSTIC TESTING

The neuro assessment and the physical examination of the patient are critical components that aid in identifying changes in function caused by stroke. Additional diagnostic testing is used to determine the type as well as the location and extent of the stroke (Jauch et al., 2013).

**CLINICAL ALERT!** Blood glucose and oxygen saturation should be measured. Both hypoglycemia and hypoxia may cause symptoms that mimic stroke and may be rapidly reversed.

A noncontrast brain computed tomography (CT) scan or brain magnetic resonance imaging (MRI) scan will give important information about the type of stroke. Serum electrolytes and blood count with platelets should be obtained if not done recently. The partial thromboplastin time (PTT)/international normalized ratio (INR) should be evaluated, especially if the patient is on anticoagulants. The radiological diagnostic testing modalities available are described in the text that follows.

## Noncontrast Head Computed Tomography Scan

The goal of the first diagnostic test is to provide data that the physician can use to determine the immediate treatment strategy. The diagnostic test that is ordered most frequently is a noncontrast head CT scan (often called a "dry" head CT). This is done immediately once neurological changes are noticed. The major goal is to determine if the stroke is ischemic (no acute changes typically seen on the CT scan) or hemorrhagic (blood is easily seen on the CT scan).

A noncontrast CT scan has the advantage of being almost universally available in hospitals. It can quickly evaluate for intracranial bleeding and rule out several other causes of symptoms (e.g., brain tumor or abscess). In addition, a noncontrast CT scan may show large arterial occlusions (hyperdense vessel sign). A CT scan in some cases may show subtle signs of an ischemic infarct within 3 hours of onset. However, it will not show small infarcts and is not a sensitive test to determine if an ischemic stroke is occurring.

## ESSENTIAL FACTS

A noncontrast head CT is considered the diagnostic test of choice when a patient experiences acute stroke symptoms.

## Computed Tomography Angiography

CT angiography (CTA) is used to evaluate noninvasively both intracranial and extracranial vessels. It involves injection of contrast dye and imaging of the arteries in the head, brain, and neck. CTA will show, with a high level of accuracy, large vessel occlusions and stenosis. However, it provides a static image, so it is not useful to show the rate or direction of blood flow.

## Diffusion-Weighted Magnetic Resonance Imaging

Standard MRI is not sensitive to ischemic changes, but diffusion-weighted imaging (DWI) is the most sensitive and specific imaging technique for an acute brain infarct. It is possible to see an area of infarction within minutes of symptom onset and to determine the size, site, and age of the infarct. In addition, DWI may show areas of irreversible infarct and regions of salvageable brain tissue (penumbra). Large artery occlusions (artery susceptibility sign) may be seen using DWI more reliably than on CT scan. However, the use of MRI is limited by cost, availability, relatively long duration of the test, increased issues with motion artifact, and additional patient contraindications.

## Magnetic Resonance Angiography

Intracranial MR angiography (MRA) is used in conjunction with brain MRI to guide decision making in acute stroke. Similar to CTA, MRA involves injecting contrast dye and imaging the arteries of the head, brain, and neck. MRA may be used to identify proximal large-vessel occlusions but is not helpful in identifying distal or branch occlusions. As noted, use of MRI is limited by availability, cost, test duration, motion artifact, and patient contraindications.

## Brain Perfusion Studies

Brain perfusion imaging, using either CT or perfusion-weighted MRI, provides information about cerebral hemodynamics (cerebral blood flow, cerebral blood volume, and mean transit time) and can show the area of ischemic penumbra. This is the area of tissue with reversible ischemia that can be saved if blood flow can be restored. These studies can also show areas that are irreversibly infarcted. These findings can be used to guide treatment

**TABLE 14.2 Functional Anatomy of the Brain**

| Lobe | Functions |
| --- | --- |
| Frontal | Higher mental functions<br>Concentration<br>Abstract thinking<br>Foresight and judgment<br>Inhibition<br>Memory<br>Personality<br>Affect<br>Voluntary motor function |
| Temporal | Hearing<br>Comprehension of spoken language (dominant hemisphere)<br>Visual, olfactory, and auditory perception<br>Memory<br>Learning and intellect<br>Emotion |
| Parietal | Sensory perception of touch, pain, temperature, position, pressure, and vibration<br>Body awareness<br>Sensory interpretation |
| Occipital | Visual perception and interpretation<br>Control of some visual and ocular movement reflexes |

decisions for the patient, such as whether to attempt to reperfuse the artery supplying the affected area. There are advantages and disadvantages to using CT versus MRI for perfusion studies. However, CT perfusion is more widely available and has fewer contraindications.

It is important to keep in mind that not all of the tests described here are available at all hospitals. Also, MRI is not an option for patients with epicardial pacing wires; those requiring circulatory support from intraaortic balloon pump, ventricular assist, or other devices; or for many patients with a permanent pacemaker.

▶ **NURSING IMPLICATIONS:** When the area of infarction or bleeding is detectable by imaging, it is important to note the size and location. This information will help determine what symptoms will be experienced as well as the patient's long-term outcome. See Table 14.2 for a list of what functions are controlled by various areas of the brain.

## Ischemic Stroke

In the general population, approximately 85% of strokes are ischemic strokes. In the cardiac surgery population, perioperative strokes are almost exclusively ischemic. Ischemic strokes often occur as a result of emboli dislodged during surgery. Atherosclerotic plaque or clots may break loose during surgical manipulation. In addition, debris and air from the surgical field may escape the filtering process and enter the circulation. Any of these emboli in the arterial circulation may travel easily into the brain through the internal carotid arteries, which are the first to branch off of the aorta and create a straight path to the brain (Figure 14.1).

In addition, atrial fibrillation is common after cardiac surgery and is a major risk factor for ischemic stroke. (See Chapters 7 and 13 for a description of atrial fibrillation and strategies to reduce the risk of a thromboembolic event.) Other possible causes of ischemic injury to the brain include hypotension or low flow states in the presence of preexisting atherosclerosis of cerebral or carotid arteries.

**CLINICAL ALERT!** Maintaining an adequate cardiac output following cardiac surgery may decrease ischemic brain injury in patients with cerebral or carotid atherosclerosis.

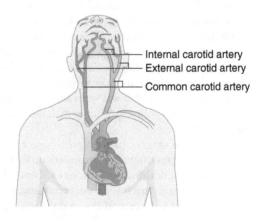

Internal carotid artery
External carotid artery
Common carotid artery

**FIGURE 14.1** Carotid arteries.

As many as 60% of strokes discovered in the first few days following cardiac surgery are complete at the time of evaluation (i.e., ischemic damage has already been done) and are not eligible for revascularization (Sila, 2012). For ischemic strokes that are still evolving, revascularization can limit the ischemic damage and improve long-term outcomes and quality of life. Administration of tissue plasminogen activator (tPA) within 3 hours (and in some cases up to 4.5 hours) of symptom onset to restore blood flow is standard treatment for ischemic stroke. However, thrombolytic therapy in cardiac surgery patients is limited by recent major surgery and use of anticoagulants, greatly increasing bleeding risk. Since major surgery within the previous 14 days is a relative exclusion to administering tPA, it is not frequently considered after cardiac surgery. In addition, myocardial infarction within the previous 3 months is also a relative contraindication to tPA administration. However, if the patient is experiencing an ischemic stroke and there is brain tissue that may be saved by revascularization, it may be considered.

Mechanical revascularization and intraarterial thrombolysis are possible in select patients after cardiac surgery. For these patients in whom an occluded cerebral vessel has been located on CTA, MRA, or traditional angiography, an interventional radiologist can attempt to physically remove the clot or embolic material,The concept is the same as removal of a clot from a coronary artery in a patient experiencing an acute ST segment elevation myocardial infarction (STEMI). Clot removal from a cerebral artery is typically performed in an interventional radiology suiteat an experienced stroke center with qualified interventional radiologists and nurses to care for the patient. Another option is an intraarterial tPA infusion. This involves the infusion of tPA in the cerebral artery next to the occlusion to break up a clot blocking blood flow to the brain. In the few cases described in the literature of intraarterial tPA administration to patients immediately post–cardiac surgery, bleeding risk was somewhat increased (Sila, 2012). However, there is not enough evidence to determine exactly what the risk would be.

Because many cardiac surgery patients who have a stroke are not eligible to receive interventional or thrombolytic treatment, it is sometimes assumed that nothing can be done for them. Although it may be true that, for some patients, no interventions can restore blood flow to the area of ischemia in the brain, there are other treatments for ischemic stroke that are aimed at prevention of secondary injury. These important interventions have a huge impact on long-term survival and functional outcomes for these patients. Prevention of secondary injury is described in detail later in this chapter.

## Hemorrhagic Stroke

Hemorrhagic stroke in the week following cardiac surgery is rare and is usually the result of a hemorrhagic conversion of an ischemic stroke. Bleeding in this case usually occurs at or near the site of the ischemic injury (intracranial hemorrhage). Due to the large amounts of anticoagulants given prior to surgery (e.g., during cardiac catheterization or treatment of myocardial infarction) and during surgery (e.g., heparinization for cardiopulmonary bypass, anticoagulation in cases of atrial fibrillation), bleeding may occur in other locations. Subarachnoid hemorrhage may occur, especially in patients who may have undetected aneurysms. Subdural hematomas, although rare, also may occur. Table 14.3 outlines features of these types of hemorrhagic stroke.

If hemorrhagic stroke is noted in a cardiac surgery patient, any anticoagulation must be aggressively reversed. Diagnostic testing as previously described will determine the location and extent of the bleeding. If the cause of the hemorrhagic stroke is a ruptured aneurysm, coiling or clipping may be attempted to stop the bleeding. Coiling of an aneurysm is a catheter-based intervention

### TABLE 14.3 Types of Hemorrhagic Stroke

| Type | Description |
|------|-------------|
| Intracerebral hemorrhage (ICH) | • Bleeding in the brain tissue; may be a result of hemorrhagic conversion if an ischemic stroke<br>• May occur in any area of the brain<br>• Severity and symptoms experienced depend on the size and location of the bleed<br>• Larger amounts of blood displace larger amounts of brain tissue, causing more damage |
| Subarachnoid hemorrhage (SAH) | • Bleeding in the subarachnoid space<br>• Often the result of a ruptured aneurysm<br>• Often causes vasospasm of cerebral arteries |
| Subdural hematoma (SDH) | • Bleeding in the dural space<br>• Often the result of trauma (fall that involves hitting the head) |

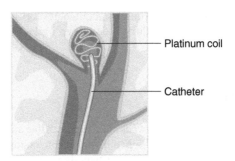

**FIGURE 14.2** Coiling of an aneurism.

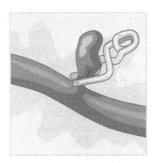

**FIGURE 14.3** Clipping of an aneurysm.

that may be performed in an interventional radiology suite (Figure 14.2). Clipping requires surgical intervention in an operating room (Figure 14.3). If the bleed is large and is compressing a large amount of brain tissue, surgical intervention to evacuate the blood may be required. Other treatment involves prevention of secondary injury.

## *ESSENTIAL FACTS*

Stroke after cardiac surgery is almost exclusively ischemic in nature. Patients who experience stroke symptoms should receive immediate diagnostic workup and be evaluated for the possibility of revascularization to limit the damage to the brain.

# PREVENTION OF SECONDARY INJURY

No matter the type of stroke or the treatment that occurred for the stroke, the patient will need specific interventions to prevent secondary injury to the brain. Secondary injury is damage that occurs to brain tissue due to processes initiated as a result of the stroke. For example, biochemical damage occurring to brain tissue as a result of ischemia can lead to brain edema, which increases pressure inside the skull and results in additional damage or even death. The irritation of blood in the subarachnoid space due to hemorrhage often leads to vasospasm, which causes additional damage in the brain due to a decrease in blood flow in the brain. The goal is to limit damage to the brain, so it is critical to be aware of and prevent the mechanisms of secondary injury.

## ESSENTIAL FACTS

For many cardiac surgery patients who experience a stroke, revascularization is not possible. However, preventing secondary injury as a result of the stroke is a critical way nurses can improve the long-term outcomes for these patients.

Prevention of secondary injury involves a number of nursing interventions, most initiated by physician order. Frequent neuro checks are important to monitor for any changes from the patient's new baseline neurological status. The new baseline is the patient's neuro assessment post-stroke. A change from this baseline may indicate that further damage is occurring in the brain. If this is suspected, additional diagnostic testing (typically CT or MRI) will usually be ordered.

Hypotension, hypoxia, and hypoglycemia are dangerous to the injured brain because needed nutrients do not reach the tissue in sufficient quantities to maintain functioning. On the other hand, fever, seizures, and hyperglycemia all increase the metabolic demand of the brain tissue and similarly may lead to issues with maintaining functioning (Hemphill, Andrews, & De Georgia, 2011). Hypovolemia may predispose a patient to hypoperfusion and may exacerbate the ischemic injury. It is important to maintain euvolemia in these patients. Hypervolemia (by flooding the patient with fluids) as a treatment strategy for stroke is no longer recommended.

# Hypoxia

Prevention of hypoxia is important in stroke patients. Hypoxia appears frequently after stroke, especially in patients with cardiac or pulmonary disease. Stroke often alters the level of consciousness and predisposes patients to partial airway obstruction, hypoventilation, aspiration, and atelectasis (Jauch et al., 2013). Oxygen should be administered to keep the oxygen saturation level at greater than 94%.

**CLINICAL ALERT!** Patients experiencing a stroke may be unable to maintain or protect the airway due to a decrease in level of consciousness or dysfunction of muscles that control swallowing. Intubation should be considered for these patients.

## Hypoglycemia and Hyperglycemia

Both hypoglycemia and hyperglycemia should be avoided, since both can lead to further damage to brain tissue. Hypoglycemia during the acute phase of a stroke is rare in the absence of diabetic medications but must be treated immediately to prevent further damage to brain tissue. Hyperglycemia during the acute stroke period has been shown to lead to worse outcomes, including increased infarct size (Jauch et al., 2013). The guidelines suggest maintaining blood glucose within a target range of 140 to 180 mg/dL.

## Fever

Approximately 30% of patients with stroke experience a fever greater than 99.7°F (37.6°C; Jauch et al., 2013). Fever must be aggressively treated, as the increase in metabolism may increase ischemia. Acetaminophen, cooling blankets, or intravascular cooling devices may be used to maintain normothermia. When cooling measures are used to treat fever, shivering often occurs, which increases body temperature and metabolic demand. Normothermia must be maintained but shivering must be avoided. One method used to prevent or stop shivering is the use of counter-warming. If using an intravascular cooling catheter, a warming blanket can be placed over the top of the patient. In addition, several medications may be used to stop shivering, including acetaminophen (Tylenol), meperidine (Demerol), buspirone (Buspar), propofol (Diprivan), dexmedetomidine (Precedex), and paralytics in severe cases.

# Seizures

Ischemia and other damage to brain tissue may also predispose patients to seizures. Depending on the size and location of the injury, anticonvulsants may be routinely ordered. Patients must be monitored closely for seizure activity. Seizures must be reported to the physician and treated aggressively to minimize further injury to the brain.

## Hypertension and Intracranial Pressure Changes

Stroke patients are at risk for increases in intracranial pressure (ICP), which may result from edema secondary to the ischemic insult or from hemorrhagic conversion (i.e., bleeding after an ischemic stroke). Because the volume in the skull is fixed, when there is an increase in brain tissue (edema), blood volume (bleeding), or cerebral spinal fluid, ICP increases unless one of the other components decreases. This is called the Monro-Kellie hypothesis. When the ICP increases, blood flow is reduced in the cerebral arteries (cerebral perfusion pressure [CPP]), which may further ischemic injury. The following formula is used to calculate CPP:

$$CPP = MAP - ICP$$

If ICP increases, mean arterial pressure (MAP) must increase or blood flow to the brain will eventually stop. Thus, maintaining the patient's blood pressure at a level high enough to ensure adequate CPP is critical.

▶ **NURSING IMPLICATIONS:** It is critical for the nurse to understand the blood pressure goal for each patient and keep the blood pressure within goal to maintain cerebral perfusion pressure.

Blood pressure is typically high during the 24 hours following an acute ischemic stroke. The current recommendation for patients in general is not to lower the blood pressure during this time unless it is over 220/120 mmHg. However, the guidelines acknowledge that some conditions coexisting with stroke, such as recent cardiac surgery, will necessitate a lower blood pressure. The current guidelines state that the best clinical judgment of the physician should guide the decision about what the target blood pressure should be (Jauch et al., 2013). Maintaining a blood pressure higher than is typically desirable for cardiac patients and avoiding hypotension are critical to maintaining blood flow in the brain. Vasopressors may be used as ordered by a physician to prevent hypotension.

## ESSENTIAL FACTS

> Maintaining adequate blood pressure is important to maintain blood flow to the brain and prevent ischemia. Cardiac surgeons typically prefer a lower blood pressure to prevent stress on the surgical sites. For cardiac surgery patients who experience a stroke, the nurse may need to work with the neurologist to advocate for a higher than usual blood pressure to maintain adequate CPP for the patient.

## Preventive Measures in Hemorrhagic Stroke

In addition to the preceding measures for preventing secondary injury, there are some additional considerations in patients with hemorrhagic stroke. Blood pressure is kept lower, especially in patients with an unsecured aneurysm (prior to coiling or clipping). Also, surgery may be performed either to remove blood from the brain or to remove part of the skull to allow for expansion of the brain without causing herniation (hemicraniotomy). If a hemicraniotomy is performed, the skull will be replaced once swelling decreases (either replacing the removed piece of skull or covering the area with a plate).

Unless there is a way to measure ICP with a catheter in the brain, it is difficult to know if the ICP is increasing or if other changes are occurring. Deterioration in clinical status occurs in 25% of stroke patients. In patients who experience deterioration, approximately 30% occurs due to progression of the stroke, 30% due to brain edema, 10% due to hemorrhage, and 11% due to recurrent ischemia (Jauch et al., 2013). The most important bedside tool for determining if changes are occurring in the brain (e.g., increasing ICP, extension of ischemic stroke, hemorrhagic conversion of a stroke) is the neuro assessment. Signs of increasing ICP include changes in the level of consciousness (restlessness, agitation, disorientation, or lethargy), changes to pupil size, shape or reactivity, and changes to sensory or motor function, usually on one side of the body. Other signs of increasing ICP include headache, blurred vision, diplopia, seizures, or vomiting. If these or other changes occur in the neuro assessment, a physician with neurological expertise should be notified and should order additional imaging, such as head CT scan or MRI. These scans will show whether increasing edema, shifts or displacement of brain tissue, or bleeding are present.

A careful neuro assessment is the most important tool available to the nurse to detect changes in the brain, including increases in intracranial pressure. The value of this assessment must not be underestimated.

## REDUCING OTHER COMPLICATIONS FOR STROKE PATIENTS

Infection is a concern in stroke patients, and is even more of a risk in patients who have recently had cardiac surgery. Pneumonia is an important cause of death after stroke. Development of pneumonia is associated with increased mortality and length of stay. After a stroke, patients are at high risk for aspiration. This may be due to changes in level of consciousness or to mechanical difficulties in using the muscles required for swallowing. It is critical that an evaluation of swallowing occur before anything is administered by mouth. This evaluation may be done by caregivers at the bedside using a validated swallowing evaluation tool or by a speech therapist. If swallowing is impaired, a nasogastric tube or nasoduodenal tube should be inserted to administer oral medications and nutrition until swallowing is restored. Patients who have long-term difficulties with swallowing after a stroke may require a percutaneous endoscopic gastrostomy (PEG) tube.

*ESSENTIAL FACTS*

Aspiration after stroke is a serious concern. A bedside swallowing evaluation or evaluation by a speech therapist must be done before anything is administered by mouth, including any ordered medications.

Urinary tract infections (UTIs) are common after stroke and may lead to worse outcomes. The onset of fever should prompt caregivers to search for possible sources of infection, including pneumonia and UTI. Indwelling urinary catheters should be removed as soon as the patient is medically and neurologically stable.

Patients with large strokes and with right hemispheric strokes are at risk for developing myocardial ischemia, congestive heart failure, atrial fibrillation, and significant arrhythmias (Jauch et al., 2013). Cardiac surgery patients are already at risk for these complications. Caution must be used when administering anticoagulants if any of these complications occur in patients with hemorrhagic stroke.

Pulmonary embolism accounts for 10% of deaths after acute stroke (Jauch et al., 2013), so prevention of deep vein thrombosis (DVT) and pulmonary embolism is important. Early mobility, use of sequential compression devices, and pharmacological prevention strategies should all be used, when possible. Barriers to these preventative strategies exist in the cardiac surgery population, such as difficulty mobilizing due to various drains and devices and contraindication to sequential compression on the leg from which the saphenous vein was removed. In addition, patients with hemorrhagic stroke should not receive antithrombotics for DVT prophylaxis until cessation of bleeding has been determined (Morgenstern et al., 2010). However, any preventative measures that are possible should be used diligently. Use of subcutaneous anticoagulants is particularly important in this population, once it is safe to administer them.

## REHABILITATION AND LONG-TERM RECOVERY

Cardiac surgery patients who experience a stroke in the perioperative period will have a longer and more difficult recovery than those who have not experienced this complication. Rehabilitation after cardiac surgery will be discussed in Chapter 16. Rehabilitation after stroke is critical to improving long-term functioning and quality of life.

It is important to include family members early in decision making and treatment planning. This can be an extremely stressful time for family. Although stroke is discussed with patients when reviewing the risks and benefits of surgery, the occurrence of stroke during or after surgery is an unexpected event. Family members need education about any available community resources. In general, family members are better able to deal with physical deficits than with cognitive deficits or changes in personality (Duncan et al., 2005). There is some evidence that family and caregivers have increased rates of depression in the post-stroke period.

Rehabilitation after stroke involves a multidisciplinary approach. It begins in the hospital and often continues in a rehabilitation facility. Physical therapists mobilize patients and teach patients and families about strategies for exercise and mobilization after discharge. Early mobilization, as soon as the patient is medically stable, is critical to prevent complications such as DVT, skin breakdown, pneumonia, and constipation. Early mobilization has been shown to improve time to recovery, decrease length of stay in the intensive care unit and hospital,and improve functional outcome (Duncan et al., 2005). Speech and occupational therapists teach patients and families how to perform activities of daily living (ADL) and provide tips and devices to help overcome physical deficits as a result of the stroke. Social workers or other mental health practitioners may be called in to help patients and families deal with the physical and emotional or personality changes that have occurred. Education should also occur on sexual functioning. These issues are important to patients and their partners and are often not adequately addressed. The most important message is that sexual activity is not contraindicated after stroke. However, both parties need to recognize and adjust for the potential effects of motor, sensory, and self-esteem difficulties.

In addition, as discussed in Chapter 16, rehabilitation for stroke involves secondary prevention of stroke (treatments and lifestyle modifications to prevent a recurrent stroke). Patients with athero-sclerotic cardiac disease also need treatments to prevent recurrent cardiac events. This includes antiplatelet therapy, hypertension control, consideration of angiotensin-converting enzyme (ACE) inhibitors, lipid-lowering therapy even in the setting of normal low-density lipoprotein cholesterol, exercise, and smoking cessa-tion (Duncan et al, 2005).

Patients with a severe stroke, who are maximally dependent for ADL, or who have a poor prognosis for functional recovery are not eligible for rehabilitation. The family should be taught how to care for the patient or should receive counseling on the benefits of nursing home placement for long-term care (Duncan et al., 2005).

## ESSENTIAL FACTS

Routine neuro assessments are critical in patients after cardiac surgery. The assessment should be compared to the baseline neuro assessment to evaluate for changes. If changes are noted, a neurologist should be consulted and diagnostic testing (CT or MRI) should be done. If it is deter-mined that the patient is having a stroke, the patient should be treated as aggressively as possible to minimize damage to the brain and poor outcomes. Care should be taken to pre-vent secondary injury to the brain. Consideration of improv-ing long-term outcomes and of rehabilitation should begin as soon as the patient is medically stable.

# REFERENCES

Duncan, P. W., Zorowitz, R., Bates, B., Choi, J. Y., Glasberg, J. J., Graham, G. D., . . . Reker, D. (2005). Management of adult stroke rehabilitation care: A clinical practice guideline. *Stroke, 36,* e100–e143.

Go, A. S., Mozaffarian, D., Rojer, V. L., Benjamin, E. J., Berry, J. D., Borden, W. B. . . . American Heart Association Statistical Committee and Stroke Statistics Subcommittee. (2013). Heart disease and stroke statistics—2013 update: A report from the American Heart Association. *Circulation, 127,* e6–e245.

Hemphill, J. C., Andrews, P., & De Georgia, M. (2011). *Multimodal monitoring and neurocritical care bioinformatics: Secondary brain injury.* Retrieved from http://www.medscape.org/viewarticle/745947_2

Hillis, L. D., Smith, P. K., Anderson, J. L., Bittl, J. A., Bridges, C. R., Byrne, J. G., . . . Winniford, M. D. (2011). 2011 ACCF/AHA guideline for coronary artery bypass graft surgery: A report of the American College of Cardiology Foundation/American Heart Association Task Force on Practice Guidelines. *Journal of the American College of Cardiology, 48,* e123–e210.

Jauch, E. C., Saver, J. L., Adams, H. P,. Jr., Bruno, A., Connors, J. J., Demaerschalk, B. M., . . . Council on Clinical Cardiology. (2013). Guidelines for the early management of patients with acute ischemic stroke: A guideline for healthcare professionals from the American Heart Association/American Stroke Association. *Stroke, 44,* 870–947.

Morgenstern, L. B., Hemphill, J. C., III, Anderson, C., Becker, K., Broderick, J. P., Connelly, E. S., Jr., . . . American Heart Association Stroke Council and Council on Cardiovascular Nursing. (2010). Guidelines for the management of spontaneous intracerebral hemorrhage: A guideline for healthcare professionals from the American Heart Association/American Stroke Association. *Stroke, 41,* 2108–2129.

Sila, C. (2012). Neurologic complications of cardiac surgery. In E. Manno (Ed.), *Emergency management in neurocritical care.* West Sussex, UK: John Wiley & Sons.

PART

V

# Long-Term Recovery

# Discharge

*Discharge is an important part of a patient's hospital stay. Arrangements made for care at home and information relayed to patients and families can make the difference between a successful recovery and serious complications. The discharge process should begin early in the hospital stay, so that it is not left for the discharging nurse to attempt to make all arrangements and complete all discharge teaching on the day of discharge. This allows for the smoothest discharge and the most retention of material by the patient.*

In this chapter, you will learn:

1. How to prepare a patient for discharge
2. What information should be relayed to patients and families to ensure a successful recovery at home
3. Follow-up necessary after discharge

## PREPARING A PATIENT FOR DISCHARGE

Discharge from the hospital can be a frightening time for patients. They have just undergone major surgery. They have been closely monitored since surgery but are now going home with no monitoring. It is not uncommon for patients to experience separation anxiety and for both patients and family members to experience difficulty dealing with minor problems. Discharge instructions after cardiac surgery are lengthy and complex. How discharge teaching is delivered makes a huge difference in retention, adherence to instructions, and anxiety at discharge.

## ESSENTIAL FACTS

Patients and families may experience fear and separation anxiety as they are discharged from the hospital.

## Delivering Information Necessary for Discharge

Patients only retain a small fraction of the education they receive at discharge. Several steps may be taken to improve retention. Information should be delivered in small amounts. Discharge teaching must be started early in the hospital stay, so that small amounts may be discussed at a time. (See Table 15.1 for suggestions for combining patient teaching with routine care.)

The information given to patients should be in terms the patient can understand. This requires an assessment of the patient's educational level and language abilities. Printed materials should be used along with verbal instructions, so patients

---

### TABLE 15.1 Suggestions for Combining Patient Teaching with Routine Care

- Begin by asking the patient questions to determine knowledge level (e.g., "Can you tell me why the doctor prescribed aspirin for you?")
- Ask the patient to demonstrate specific skills (incision care, use of incentive spirometer) to determine skill level (e.g., "Show me how you were taught to wash your incisions.")
- Every time a medication is administered, review indication and side effects
- Educate about taking a pulse rate and temperature while performing vital signs
- Provide teaching on signs of infection while examining incisions during a physical assessment (e.g., "I am looking at your incisions for any signs of infection. What are the signs of infection? Do you see any when you look at your incisions?")
- Teach patients to perform their own incision care while bathing them
- While walking a patient, talk about activity after discharge
- At mealtime, educate the patient about a heart-healthy diet

and family members can reference the material later. Whenever possible, various media, such as videos, drawings, or computer programs, should be used in addition to verbal instructions and printed materials. Those who will be caring for patients at home should be involved in the educational sessions.

When teaching patients and family members, questions should be encouraged. To assess how well transfer of knowledge has occurred, the patient should be asked to repeat or demonstrate what was taught. This is known as the "teach-back" method. Asking "Do you understand?" is not an effective way to gauge understanding, because many patients will answer in the affirmative even if they do not understand.

Non-English speakers and patients for whom English is not the native language are especially difficult to teach. Every effort should be made to provide translators as necessary. Family members should be engaged in the teaching process. Printed materials in the patient's native language should be used whenever possible.

## ESSENTIAL FACTS

Teaching should be done in a way that each patient can understand using as many different modalities as possible. Patients should be asked to explain what has been taught to ensure understanding.

## Discharge Teaching

### Medications

Patients should be sent home with a complete list of medications. This includes medications that they were taking prior to surgery that are to be continued, as well as new medications prescribed after surgery. Newly prescribed medications will require a prescription to be sent home with the patient. It is crucial for patient safety that medications be carefully reviewed prior to discharge. These efforts at medication reconciliation will prevent patient confusion about what medications to take at home.

After coronary artery bypass grafting, patients are prescribed aspirin indefinitely to reduce the incidence of graft failure. Patients who have had a myocardial infarction or have left ventricular dysfunction may be sent home with a beta-blocker or an angiotensin-converting enzyme (ACE) inhibitor. Oral pain medications are usually prescribed. Other medications, which may be prescribed based on the patient's history and hospital course, include diuretics and medications to control specific cardiovascular risk factors. Many patients who have undergone valve replacement are sent home on warfarin (Coumadin). If a patient received a mechanical valve, warfarin must be taken indefinitely. If a tissue valve was implanted, warfarin is prescribed for a few months or not at all.

By the time of discharge, patients should be familiar with the medications they will be taking at home and should know what they are for and their potential major side effects. This is important for improving adherence to taking the prescribed medications.

## ESSENTIAL FACTS

> Patients should receive teaching about medications throughout their hospital stay so that, at discharge, they already understand the indications and side effects of most of the medications they will take at home.

### Diet

While recovering from surgery, many patients have a poor appetite, which can take several weeks to return. Many have a diminished or absent sense of taste for several weeks. Some patients even feel nauseated at the sight or smell of food. During this initial period, the physician may not restrict the diet because patients often struggle to take in enough calories for healing. Patients should be informed that their appetite and sense of taste will return. Patients should also be aware that, once appetite returns, they should follow a diet low in saturated fat and cholesterol and low in sodium. Patients should have a consultation with a dietician prior to discharge to review their ordered diet.

### Activity

Patients should slowly increase their activity. Walking is an excellent activity after cardiac surgery. Patients with a midline sternotomy should not lift more than 10 lbs. for 6 weeks after surgery.

Also, activities involving pushing or pulling, such as mowing the lawn, moving furniture, or vacuuming, should be avoided for 6 weeks, as this places strain on the sternotomy incision. It is important that patients balance activity with rest. Patients should rest between activities, take naps as needed, and wait 30 minutes after meals before exercising.

After cardiac surgery, patients should not drive for 6 weeks due to strain on the sternotomy incision, slowed reflexes, and decreased range of motion. Sexual activity may be resumed once patients feel ready. Usually this is in about 2 to 4 weeks after surgery. Depending on their profession, patients may be able to return to light work after 6 to 12 weeks. Patients should be instructed to consult with the surgeon before returning to work.

After a minimally invasive procedure or one with small thoracotomy incisions, there are relatively few physical limitations. The physician should prescribe an activity level appropriate for the patient.

Patients should learn how to take their own pulse. While exercising and performing other activities, the heart rate should be kept no higher than 30 beats per minute above the resting pulse.

## ESSENTIAL FACTS

After cardiac surgery, most patients are restricted to lifting no more that 10 lbs. and are not allowed to drive for 6 weeks. Physical activity is beneficial and should be increased slowly with rest periods in between activities.

### Incision Care

Care of the incisions after discharge plays a large role in proper healing and prevention of infection. Patients should be able to demonstrate proper incisional care by the time of discharge from the hospital. Incisions should be washed daily with mild soap and water. A soapy hand or washcloth may be rubbed directly over the incision, but vigorous scrubbing should be avoided. Patients should avoid soaking in a bathtub until incisions are healed. Steristrips will fall off on their own or may be removed after 7 days. Staples will need to be removed at the doctor's office or by a visiting nurse. Lotions, oils, or powders should not be applied to the incisions unless prescribed by the surgeon.

If vein grafts were taken from the legs, additional instructions should be given. The affected leg may be more swollen than the one without an incision. Patients should keep the affected leg elevated to the level of the heart whenever sitting to minimize swelling. Edema negatively affects incisional healing by reducing blood flow to the incision. Patients should also avoid crossing their legs or standing or sitting in one position for long periods of time.

## ESSENTIAL FACTS

Patients should wash incisions daily with mild soap and water and keep legs with incisions elevated to heart level to minimize edema.

### Infection

Patients should be taught signs of infection so they can notify the physician early. Patients should be instructed to report increased tenderness, redness or swelling of incisions, new or increased drainage from incisions, or fever.

### Prophylactic Antibiotics

Patients who underwent a valve replacement need antibiotics before undergoing dental work, including teeth cleaning. Other patients who need prophylactic antibiotics due to high risk of contracting bacterial endocarditis include those with a history of endocarditis and those with prosthetic grafts. This is due to the risk that bacteria, released into the bloodstream during manipulation of the gums, will become lodged in the prosthetic material and cause endocarditis. The American Heart Association has published recommendations regarding antibiotics to use for prophylaxis prior to dental procedures (Wilson et al., 2007).

## Discharge Follow-Up

Upon discharge, patients need to understand the plan for followup. They should have a scheduled appointment with the cardiac surgeon. They should also be instructed to see their cardiologist within a few weeks after discharge. Patients should understand who they should call for what problems and be given phone numbers for the offices of the surgeon and cardiologist. Any other available resources, such as an advice nurse or cardiac rehabilitation program, should be given to patients.

Patients being discharged on warfarin (Coumadin) should receive extensive education on the indication for, and side effects of, the drug. They should receive a visit from a dietician to explain dietary restrictions. They should go home with a plan for follow-up laboratory testing to monitor the international normalized ratio (INR). Either a specialized clinic or the physician's office should be responsible for monitoring lab results and ensuring that the patient's INR is at a safe level.

## ESSENTIAL FACTS

Patients need to have clear instructions on when and with whom to follow-up after discharge. Patients on warfarin (Coumadin) need to have a specific physician or clinic to follow their lab results.

## OTHER CONSIDERATIONS

As hospital stays become shorter and patients are discharged sooner, many patients are still debilitated or have special needs when it is time for discharge. Upon discharge after cardiac surgery, most patients will need help at home. They should have a family member or friend at home for at least the first week, ideally longer. This should help to allay some of the patient's fears and provide someone to assist in the care of the patient and call for help if needed.

Some patients will need more care than can be provided at home. Patients who are debilitated or who need extensive physical therapy will need to go to a skilled nursing or rehabilitation facility prior to going home. Also, patients in need of intravenous antibiotics or extensive wound care may need to spend time in a skilled nursing facility prior to going home. Patients with minor needs may be able to go home with support of a visiting nurse. The patient, family, physician, case manager, nurse, and physical therapist should be involved in making the decision about discharge needs. Arrangements should be made as early as possible in the patient's hospital stay.

## ESSENTIAL FACTS

Patients should have help at home or spend time in a skilled nursing or rehabilitation facility prior to going home. Discharge needs should be determined early by the health care team in collaboration with the patient and family.

## BIBLIOGRAPHY

Bojar, R. M. (2011). *Manual of perioperative care in adult cardiac surgery* (5th ed.). West Sussex, UK: Wiley-Blackwell.

Wilson, W., Taubert, K. A., Gewitz, M., Lockhart, P. B., Baddour, L. M., Levison, M., . . . Durack, D. T. (2007). Prevention of infective endocarditis: Guidelines from the American Heart Association. *Circulation, 116*(15), 1736–1754.

Woods, S. L., Froelicher, E. S. S., Motzer, S. U., & Bridges, E. J. (Eds.). (2010). *Cardiac nursing* (6th ed.). Philadelphia, PA: Wolters Kluwer/ Lippincott Williams & Wilkins.

# 16

## Cardiac Rehabilitation

*Recovery from cardiac surgery is not over when a patient is discharged from the hospital. Most patients have a long recovery ahead of them. Many institutions have cardiac rehabilitation programs to assist patients in their recovery and return to health. The goal of these programs is to not only assist in recovery from surgery but also to decrease the risk of future cardiovascular disease by improving risk factors.*

In this chapter, you will learn:

1. The four phases of cardiac rehabilitation programs
2. Risk factors targeted in secondary prevention programs, including cardiac rehabilitation programs

## CARDIAC REHABILITATION

Cardiac rehabilitation programs are multidisciplinary programs designed to reduce the risk of cardiovascular events. These programs are considered secondary prevention programs since they are designed to reduce the risk of events, such as myocardial infarction or stroke, in patients who are known to have cardiovascular disease. (Primary prevention refers to the attempt to prevent a disease from occurring in the first place.) Usually, insurance must cover the cost of cardiac rehabilitation for patients to be able to participate.

Cardiac rehabilitation programs and other secondary prevention programs begin with an extensive baseline patient assessment. These programs contain several core components designed to reduce cardiovascular risk, promote healthy behaviors, encourage exercise, and reduce disability in patients with cardiovascular disease. The components focused on by these programs include nutritional counseling, risk factor management, physical activity counseling, and exercise training. Risk factor management involves optimizing treatment of lipids, blood pressure, weight, diabetes mellitus, and smoking. Finally, cardiac rehabilitation programs use psychosocial interventions designed to improve factors such as depression, marital or family distress, and substance abuse, which interfere with health. Cardiac rehabilitation programs consist of four phases.

## ESSENTIAL FACTS

Cardiac rehabilitation programs are designed to improve health and prevent progression of cardiovascular disease.

## Phase I

Phase I of cardiac rehabilitation begins in the hospital after a cardiac event (myocardial infarction, stent placement, or cardiac surgery). This phase consists of supervised exercise and education about medication, diet, exercise, and reducing risk factors for coronary artery disease. Often, the education consists of a structured class that patients and family members attend prior to discharge.

## Phase II

Patients enter phase II of cardiac rehabilitation between 2 and 6 weeks after discharge. A physician referral is required. The goal of phase II is to return patients to a normal active life. This is accomplished by improving functional capacity and endurance, providing education about lifestyle changes, increasing activity or exercise while reducing fear, and assisting with psychosocial adjustments after surgery.

The major emphasis of phase II is education, which may consist of individual or group classes. Family members are encouraged to attend with patients. Education topics include medications, lifestyle changes, goal setting, nutrition, stress management, and safely performing various activities. Most phase II programs meet for 1 hour three or more times per week for 12 weeks. Supervised exercise sessions include monitoring of telemetry and blood pressure.

## Phase III

Phase III of cardiac rehabilitation is a continuation of phase II; however, patients may be referred by a physician into phase III without having gone through phase II of the program. Phase III is usually entered 6 to 14 weeks after discharge. The goals of phase III are to provide ongoing supervised exercise, offer continuing support for lifestyle changes, achieve independence, and prevent progression of cardiovascular disease. Supervised exercise takes place three or more times per week, with blood pressure and telemetry monitoring.

## Phase IV

Phase IV of cardiac rehabilitation is for patients who have completed any of the previous phases. It involves continuing work on lifestyle changes. Exercise continues three or more times per week with minimal supervision.

### ESSENTIAL FACTS

Cardiac rehabilitation programs have four phases. Phase I takes place in the hospital prior to discharge. Phases II and III may be entered with a physician referral without having gone through previous phases. Phase IV is a continuation of work done in one of the first three phases.

# SECONDARY PREVENTION

One of the goals of cardiac rehabilitation is secondary prevention. The aim of secondary prevention programs is to prevent progression of cardiovascular disease in patients who have already been found to have cardiovascular disease by optimizing modifiable risk factors.

## Diet

A dietary assessment is completed, including current weight and nutritional status. An individualized plan is developed based on each patient's needs. A diet plan is developed, consisting of a diet low in saturated fat and cholesterol and taking into account any other factors, such as diabetes, hypertension, heart failure, or cultural preferences. Patients and families are educated on the plan and taught how to change eating patterns to improve their health.

## Blood Pressure Management

Blood pressure is assessed on at least two separate occasions. The goal is to maintain a blood pressure of less than 140/90 mmHg or less than 130/80 mmHg for patients with chronic kidney disease, diabetes, or heart failure. If blood pressure is between 120 and 130 mmHg systolic or 80 and 89 mmHg diastolic, lifestyle modifications to decrease blood pressure are taught and encouraged. These include regular physical activity, weight management, moderation with alcohol, and smoking cessation. Dietary interventions include sodium restriction and increased consumption of fruits, vegetables, and low-fat dairy products. For patients whose blood pressure is above goal, medications should be used in addition to lifestyle measures.

## *ESSENTIAL FACTS*

Blood pressure should be kept below 140/90 mmHg or below 130/80 mmHg for patients with chronic kidney disease, diabetes, or heart failure.

Fasting serum levels of total cholesterol, high-density lipoprotein (HDL), low-density lipoprotein (LDL), and triglycerides are measured. The goal for lipid management is to maintain an LDL level of less than 100 mg/dL. For patients at very high risk of having progression of cardiovascular disease, an LDL level of less than 70 mg/dL is often desired. To improve serum lipid levels, lifestyle change should be recommended. Therapeutic lifestyle change (TLC) is the basis for recommendations for nutritional counseling and lifestyle change. Nutritional counseling includes decreasing intake of dietary saturated fat and cholesterol, adding plant stanols/sterols and viscous fiber, and eating more omega-3 fatty acids. Other lifestyle changes recommended include weight management, exercise, smoking cessation, and moderation with alcohol.

If lifestyle changes do not cause serum lipid levels to reach goal levels, drug therapy should be initiated. There are several different classes of lipid-lowering drugs. There is much variability in patient response to these medications and each has side effects, so patient education and monitoring are required.

## ESSENTIAL FACTS

LDL cholesterol level should be kept below 100 mg/dL or below 70 mg/dL for very high-risk patients.

## Diabetes Management

For patients with diabetes, any history of diabetes complications, such as vascular disease, kidney disease, or problems with eyes or feet, are identified. Episodes of hyperglycemia or hypoglycemia are documented. The patient's treatment regimen, including medications to treat diabetes, diet, and blood glucose monitoring, is determined. Serum fasting glucose and glycosylated hemoglobin (HbA1c) levels are drawn.

The goal is to keep the serum fasting glucose level between 90 and 130 mg/dL and the HbA1c less than 7%. This is accomplished using one or more of the following measures: dietary interventions, oral medications, or insulin. Blood glucose measurements are taken prior to and after exercise in a cardiac rehabilitation program.

## *ESSENTIAL FACTS*

> To minimize progression of cardiovascular disease, serum
> fasting glucose should be between 90 and 130 mg/dL and
> HbA1c should be less than 7%.

## Tobacco Cessation

Smoking is the single most preventable cause of morbidity and
mortality and is one of the major risk factors for cardiovascular disease. Smoking cessation is a large focus for cardiac rehabilitation
and secondary prevention programs. Five interventions (known as
the five A's) have been shown to help patients quit smoking: ask,
advise, assess, assist, and arrange.

### Ask

Identify every smoker every time they are seen by a health care
professional (doctor visit, on admit to the hospital, at cardiac rehabilitation). Status of smoking should be documented for all patients (never smoked, former smoker, current smoker). A patient
who quit smoking in the last 12 months is considered a current
smoker, due to the high probability of relapse. The amount of
cigarettes smoked should be quantified by asking the number of
cigarettes smoked per day and the duration, in years, of smoking
behaviors.

### Advise

Strongly urge all smokers to quit. Smokers need a direct and strong
statement or most will continue to deny the need to quit. The message should be personalized to the patient's own health issues.

### Assess

Patient readiness to quit smoking should be determined. Patients
will only quit when they are ready and should be asked if they
are ready to quit. Patients who express that they are not willing
to try to quit should be encouraged. Review with them why quitting is relevant to them (due to their current health problems such
as cardiovascular disease, lung disease, etc.). Review the risks of

smoking and the rewards that would come with quitting. Help patients examine what the roadblocks are for them personally. Finally, remember that repetition is important and patients should hear these things at every visit. These are referred to as the five R's: relevance, risks, rewards, roadblocks, and repetition.

## Assist

Help patients who are willing to quit to set up a quit plan. This should include setting a quit date, telling friends, family, and co-workers about the intention to quit and asking for support, anticipating the challenges, and removing all tobacco products from home and work. Patients should be provided with resources and help if desired. If the patient plans to quit alone, self-help resources should be provided. If the patient decides a group cessation program would be more beneficial, a referral should be made to a group program. There are several medications that can be helpful when quitting. A knowledgeable practitioner must be involved in assisting the patient to decide which medication would be best and should monitor progress.

## Arrange

Follow-up improves smoking cessation. Follow-up with a health care provider should occur soon after the determined quit date. Frequent follow-up during the quitting process will improve the patient's ability to remain free of tobacco.

### ESSENTIAL FACTS

Smoking is one of the major modifiable risk factors for cardiovascular disease. An attempt should be made with every visit to encourage smokers to quit.

## Physical Activity and Exercise Training

Increasing physical activity is a critical aspect of secondary prevention. Physical activity level and exercise capacity at baseline are documented. Counseling is provided on how to increase physical activity on a daily basis until patients are able to accumulate 30 to 60 minutes of moderate-intensity physical activity on at least 5 days of the week. For patients who are involved in supervised exercise, an exercise prescription is made that involves aerobic and resistance training. In phases II and III of a cardiac rehabilitation program, heart rate and rhythm, any signs and symptoms of ischemia, and perceived exertion are monitored during exercise.

## *ESSENTIAL FACTS*

Patients should be encouraged to exercise for 30 to 60 minutes at least 5 days of the week.

## Psychosocial Management

Psychosocial distress is identified, as it can interfere with lifestyle changes. Depression, anxiety, anger, hostility, social isolation, marital or family distress, sexual dysfunction, and substance abuse are all identified early so interventions can take place. Individual or small group counseling is provided on adjustment to heart disease and managing stress. Family members are involved, if possible. Referral is made to a mental health provider, if necessary.

## *ESSENTIAL FACTS*

Cardiac rehabilitation is a multidisciplinary program designed to improve the health of patients by reducing cardiovascular risk factors and encouraging a healthy lifestyle.

## BIBLIOGRAPHY

Baladay, G. J., Williams, M. A., Ades, P. A., Bittner, V., Cosmos, P., Foody, J. M., . . . American Association of Cardiovascular and Pulmonary Rehabilitation. (2007). Core components of cardiac rehabilitation/secondary prevention programs: 2007 update. *Circulation, 115,* 2675–2682.

Woods, S. L., Froelicher, E. S. S., Motzer, S. U., & Bridges, E. J. (Eds.). (2010). *Cardiac nursing* (6th ed.). Philadelphia, PA: Wolters Kluwer/Lippincott Williams & Wilkins.

# Index

Note: Page numbers followed by "f" and "t" denote figures and tables, respectively.